Talking With
About Sex
Christian Perspective

BEFORE
THEY
ASK

**A GUIDE FOR
PARENTS
OF CHILDREN
FROM BIRTH
THROUGH
AGE TWELVE**

Revised and Updated

BEFORE THEY ASK
A GUIDE FOR PARENTS
OF CHILDREN FROM BIRTH
THROUGH AGE TWELVE

 Abingdon Press

05 06 07 08 — 10 9 8 7 6 5 4 3 2

MANUFACTURED IN THE UNITED STATES OF AMERICA

CONTENTS

ACKNOWLEDGMENTS

Vince Isner is a writer, video producer, and director. His company, V.I.P. Media, produces programs for non-profit and service-oriented clients, including The United Methodist Publishing House and United Methodist Communications.

Vince earned a bachelor's degree in music from Centenary College of Louisiana and a master's degree from United Theological Seminary, Dayton, Ohio, where he specialized in child development and television communications.

Vince has taught kindergarten, worked in a children's hospital, and served as a United Methodist minister to children and families. As Director of Higher Education Media Services at UMCom, he produced several videos for colleges and universities. Vince's scripts on children's issues have won both a Telly Award and the CINE Golden Eagle.

Vince and his wife have two children and live in Franklin, Tennessee.

We are grateful to **Don and Rhoda Preston**, who wrote the original *Before They Ask,* published in 1989. They did a marvelous job of equipping parents for the joy of sharing one of life's greatest miracles with their children. The revisions made for the new edition reflect changes in national statistics since the 1989 writing. Also reflected is the belief that sex should not be treated as some "special subject," but as a natural and joyful part of life.

INTRODUCTION

From the Editor

Let's face it: Sex has been around since the beginning of everything. Very little has changed since our earliest ancestors set about populating our planet. What *has* changed, however, is our thinking about sex. Next to examining a culture's religion, there is perhaps no better way to understand a culture or a people's mindset than by examining its thoughts and beliefs about sex.

For the most part Christians adopted the sexual mores of Judaism. The challenges of the time in which they lived and their determination to survive as a faith community determined their beliefs about sex. The challenge for today's society is just as critical. Those children who are ignorant of sex and sexuality are at social and physical risk. Because of the opportunities that exist to be exposed to "negative sex" via cable television and the Internet, we owe it to them to discuss sex openly and honestly.

In his book *Wishful Thinking* (Harper & Row, 1973), Frederich Buechner wrote, "Contrary to Mrs. Grundy, sex is not sin. Contrary to Hugh Hefner, it's not salvation either." Sex is a part of God's good creation. We need to overcome our discomfort in talking about it. Fred Rogers, America's favorite children's television neighbor, says, "Anything mentionable is manageable."

Sexuality begins at birth. It is a lifelong learning process and involves many questions at many times throughout life. You can't do it all in one evening. Use this book as a guide. You'll no doubt discover some things about your own beliefs that will surprise you.

Finally, talk with your children early and often. It may require some practice, but your children will thank you for it later. You will discover that your own comfort level with the topic will increase as well. Trust yourself. You are the best possible person for sharing with your children what love and healthy sexuality are all about.

CHAPTER 1

Hopes and Expectations

EXPECTANT PARENTS

The doctor leaned across his desk, took our hands, and with a bright smile exclaimed, "Congratulations, Don and Rhoda! You're going to have a baby!" His good news left us feeling dizzy with anticipation and joy.

A baby! Almost immediately we began to picture life as parents. What great hopes and dreams we had for this yet-to-be-born child! Our baby, of course, would be happy, healthy, and wholly cherished—we would be intentional about that. With a band director for a father and a piano teacher for a mother, our child would naturally be musical. We also expected that this new family member would enjoy sports, devour books, love God, and make friends easily. We pledged that our home would be free from sexual stereotypes. We filled the nursery with colorful, stimulating toys and read every book we could find on parenting—expecting our child would be exceptionally perceptive and alert.

That was twelve years ago. Our two children, Kathryn and Timothy, are now eleven and seven, and you know what? We're still expectant parents! That is, we expect so much of our son and daughter. We still hope each has a strong self-image and every chance for fulfillment. We want them to form positive relationships—to learn to give and to receive love. We are eager that they learn to think for themselves and become persons of integrity and kindness. We also expect a lot of ourselves as parents. We expect to communicate our Christian values with our children, encourage the fulfillment of their dreams, and help them learn and grow from our insights. And yes, we still find ourselves poring over books on parenting, always expecting that one day we'll know how it's done!

EXPECTATIONS AND CONCERNS ABOUT OUR CHILD'S GENDER

Before Kathryn's birth, friends would ask, "What are you hoping for—a boy or a girl?" We always gave the stock answer, "Oh, it doesn't matter. As long as it's healthy." But Rhoda secretly hoped for a girl. The idea of raising a boy frightened her. How did little boys think and feel? She wasn't sure. She had a wonderful brother, but since he was six years older, she had not known him as a little boy.

A baby girl would be different—something far less mysterious. After all, Rhoda thought, I was once a little girl. My best childhood friends were my sisters. I'm close to my own mother. I'm comfortable with being female. Raising a male child would be a journey into strange and even frightening new territory!

It's common to have such gender-related concerns. Being born a boy or a girl brings a lot of cultural baggage for both children and parents. Society often assigns a set of rights, duties, and appropriate behaviors to males and females that are unique to each gender. How a person then feels about himself or herself is influenced by those expectations.

These standards are one reason parents often prefer having children of one sex instead of the other. For example, throughout Biblical history families have desired a son to carry on the family name. Genesis 15 relates how Abram longed for a son. When God promised Abram a great reward for his faithfulness, Abram told God in no uncertain terms that God's reward would mean nothing without a son to inherit that reward.

Parents may have other reasons for preferring a child of a particular gender. For example, a woman who has felt her own opportunities denied because of her gender may prefer a son, believing that a daughter might encounter the same limitations. Likewise, a man who has been constantly pressured by his father and grandfather to excel in sports or in the family business may wish for a daughter, in hopes of breaking the chain of pressure.

Sometimes the reasons are more practical. Some parents may find it easier or less expensive to have a child of a certain sex. After the birth of her third son, our friend Jane was visited by a neighbor to offer a sympathetic ear. The neighbor was convinced that Jane would be devastated after not having at least one daughter. "Actually," Jane said, "I was relieved. I'm a expert now on boys. And besides, we won't have to buy all new baby clothes."

PARENTS' EXPECTATIONS ABOUT THEIR CHILD'S SEXUALITY

Parents are not only concerned about their child's gender role, but also about their child's sexuality as well. Sexuality refers to more than "the plumbing." It encompasses the physical and emotional aspects of being male or female. Sexuality is part of who we are as human beings. It involves our hearts and minds as well as our bodies. Our sexuality informs our ethics, colors our desires, influences our actions, and defines our relationships.

Understanding and expressing a healthy sexuality is crucial for a life of fulfillment and joy. It's what loving parents want for their children. That's why it's important to know what makes for a positive, healthy sexuality. Armed with correct knowledge parents can help their children avoid pain and confusion.

Understanding sexuality isn't easy for children. Appropriate meanings, values, actions, and feelings about sexuality must all be learned. While children gather some information in school, peer groups, Sunday school, and church, ultimately it's the parents' privilege to serve as the primary sex educators for children.

PARENTS AS THE PRIMARY SEX EDUCATORS

What does it mean for parents to teach sex education to their children? Does it mean trying to control and suppress sexual expression to ensure the child "stays out of trouble"? No. Does it mean drilling children on the facts of life? Of course not. Bombarding young children with such learning activities is neither appropriate nor helpful. That wouldn't be wise in teaching any subject, including sexuality.

On the other hand responsible parents do not postpone sex education. They also know that a "crash course" in the birds and the bees won't do the trick. Effective sex education involves building self-esteem and helping children understand and accept themselves as sexual beings. Building such a lifetime view of a child's sexuality enables the child to say "No" to sexual contact today and an enthusiastic "Yes" to an appropriate and healthy expression of his or her sexuality in the future.

Responsible sex education has several rewards. Children will grow to use their sexual knowledge in a responsible manner, making wise decisions and avoiding ignorance, misinformation, fear, and negative attitudes. Taught in an open, warm, and caring atmosphere, children see healthy relationships and appreciate the love and importance of the family.

According to The American Association of Sex Educators, Counselors and Therapists (AASECT), several topics should be included in sex education. One is human reproduction—including information about menstruation, conception, contraception, and pregnancy. Another area is an understanding of developmental changes that occur as a person grows—changes that might raise anxieties about whether or not one is normal.

Most professional sex educators agree that children should have a solid understanding of these two areas (reproduction and the physical changes of puberty) before reaching middle school. As adolescents they are then free to focus on the development of relationships, attitudes, and values. The implication here is that most parents, churches, and schools wait far too long before beginning sex education. Then, to make matters worse, the instruction in sex education often ends with the acquisition of biological facts, without giving children the assistance they need to form their own values.

LIVING DAY BY DAY

Life cannot be compartmentalized. Each part of our lives is shaped and influenced by every other part. Our experiences intertwine to shape and to form us as whole persons. An important suggestion, then, for family sex education would be this: Gain good general parenting skills. The purpose of the remainder of this chapter is to suggest what some of those general parenting skills might be and to show how each may influence our child's sexual identity.

HELPING OUR CHILDREN TO KNOW GOD

One of the privileges of Christian parenting is helping our children to know God personally. Do they know that God loves and values them? This assurance can be the foundation for a self-esteem that will enable them to love themselves. Have we helped our children discover what the Bible says about life and relationships? Its stories can guide actions and influence values. Do our sons and daughters know how to pray? Have they experienced the wisdom, peace, and power from time spent alone with God? Helping our children build a vital relationship with God means that we must talk with them about God and must also model a set of values based on our understanding of Christian love. We can make the Scriptures and prayer a natural part of our daily lives, using them as a source of wisdom and as tools for self-discipline.

FAMILY ATMOSPHERE

An important ingredient in any home is family atmosphere. How does it feel to be present in your home? Do the members of your family experience security, gentleness, caring, and intimacy? Are family members "kind to one another" (Ephesians 4:32a)? Do parents and children alike know what it means to be valued and loved? Does your family enjoy being together, so that members are comfortable and happy being part of the family? Do you experience moments of joy together? Do you have a sense of family identity and pride?

Children who know from birth what it means to be cherished and loved are apt to grow into adults who accept God's love and who extend this love to others. They will realize how important family loyalty is and will have had opportunity to practice building and sustaining joyful relationships. Such children will understand how to think in terms of "we" instead of "me" and will have had experience in demonstrating patience, flexibility, and concern for the well-being of others.

Listen to Philippians 2:1-4 and hear how Paul's words speak to the way in which Christian persons can develop a warm and loving atmosphere in their homes:

If then there is any encouragement in Christ, any consolation from love, any sharing in the Spirit, any compassion and sympathy, make my joy complete: be of the same mind, having the same love, being in full accord and of one mind. Do nothing from selfish ambition or conceit, but in humility regard others as better than yourselves. Let each of you look not to your own interests, but to the interests of others.

A Christian family who tries to reflect the love of Christ in their home will be putting this kindness, consideration, and loving unity into practice every day.

A warm family atmosphere is a safe place for learning to handle emotions. Parents who say, "It looks to me like you're feeling sad (or discouraged, excited, angry, afraid, and so forth) are teaching their children to be sensitive to the feelings of others. Adults who try to get at the root of emotions—especially those that accompany growing up—are teaching their children to be thoughtful and reasonable. They'll be better prepared to react responsibly to their own feelings, and that in turn prepares them to form healthy relationships.

The story of Nehemiah in the Bible is an example of how sensitivity to the feelings of others and the practice of emotional discipline can have a positive effect on a person's life. Nehemiah, the wine steward for Emperor Artaxerxes of Persia, was usually a happy person. Yet one day the emperor was surprised to see his servant looking sad. Nehemiah recounts the story with these words:

I had never been sad in [Artaxerxes'] presence before. So the king said to me, "Why is your face sad, since you are not sick? This can only be sadness of the heart." (Nehemiah 2:1-2, adapted)

Nehemiah was amazed that his feelings were noticed by the emperor. The emperor's sensitivity left Nehemiah free to answer, "Yes, I am unhappy." He told Artaxerxes of his grief over the destruction of Jerusalem, and together they came up with a solution. The emperor gave Nehemiah the opportunity to change the circumstances that were causing his unhappiness, granting him permission to return to Jerusalem and to oversee the rebuilding of the city. The insight and sensitivity of Artaxerxes and the willingness of Nehemiah to come to grips with his feelings give a positive model for parents and children to explore as they wrestle with their own feelings.

BUILDING SELF-ESTEEM

Families need to appreciate and to value each member. Healthy self-esteem enables a person to develop and grow psychologically, laying a foundation for success in almost every area of life. Self-esteem contributes to feelings of competence, worth, and acceptance, and enhances the formation of meaningful relationships—relationships founded on mutual love and respect. Without self-esteem it is difficult for persons to love themselves, to overcome fear of rejection or inferiority, or to accept their own limitations as well as the limitations of others. Children who have positive thoughts about themselves grow to become more positive adults!

How can we build self-esteem in our daughters and sons? We can care for their physical needs. We can let them know through our explicit words and actions that they are cherished and respected. We can say, "Let's do something together," showing our children that we value their company. We can find an hour in our busy schedule to volunteer for a school carnival or to decorate two dozen cupcakes for a Valentine party. We can give our children the freedom to be unique and not insist that they be a carbon copy of their brothers and sisters or parents. We can ask for their assistance, for their ideas, and for their opinions. We can accept their differences of opinion without feeling angry or threatened. We can give our sons and daughters a voice in family decisions, celebrate their successes, and thank them for their help. We can tell them, "What you just did made me very happy, and I appreciate you greatly." In our family, we often use memories to celebrate the uniqueness of each person. Kathy and Timothy like to look in their baby books to see the many cards of congratulation that were sent at their birth. We enjoy browsing through old photographs and saying, "Remember when you made your first soccer goal? Remember how much you loved your first kitten?" We try to make birthdays an especially happy time, and say, "Remember the year we went to the professional baseball game on your birthday? Remember your 'Sleeping Beauty' cake?" We talk about special times we have shared and encourage our children to find ways to remember their experiences and feelings—through keeping diaries or through having a dresser drawer for pictures and papers too precious to part with.

When we work at building our children's self-esteem, we are helping them know that there is something special about them that no one else can duplicate. We are reinforcing their conviction that their bodies, as well as their entire selves, are good! We believe that this realization will help our children form mature attitudes about their sexuality and prepare them to make loving, lifetime commitments when they become adults!

COMMUNICATION SKILLS

Throughout this book we will be stressing the importance of family communication. We believe that children who feel comfortable talking with their parents about fears, fantasies, hopes, and frustrations will also be open to talking about sexuality. Families that have a history of listening to one another will continue to listen when the concerns are physical changes or sexual relationships. Families that communicate will find it easier to make decisions and resolve conflicts.

To communicate effectively family members must first take time to be together. It is hard to have a relaxed conversation when no one has the time to listen. Set aside moments just to be together, to enjoy one another's company. Take the phone off the hook or plan an outing to the park. Driving in the car can provide a good opportunity to talk. Some of the simplest tasks have the potential for becoming some of your best opportunities for communication.

Many families find that it helps to be doing something together when you talk. Having a task eases self-consciousness and lessens tension, making it easier to talk. Working together also creates a feeling of support and rapport between family members—an important basis for open discussions. Just make sure you don't get so caught up in the project that you can't "bother" to talk!

Putting thoughts and feelings into words is often difficult. That's where listening becomes important. Listening helps the words to come. Listening takes energy, alertness, and concentration. A good listener is interested and shows this interest with eye contact or a smile. A good listener pays attention to what is said and notes facial expressions and tone of voice, which may give special meaning to the words. Listening gives us valuable information about one another. Listening also sends the message that the listener cares, and it makes the person who is talking feel important and accepted.

Young children often communicate more through behavior than with words. Observing children's behavior can be just as important as listening to their words. As children grow, their vocabulary will grow too. Parents can create a comfortable space for communication simply by inviting them to share: "Susie, you look sad," or "Bryan, you must be very proud to have scored the winning goal!" Once children have started to open up, parents can encourage them to keep talking by being good listeners.

Parents also need to make sure they are really hearing what their child says. Do not assume that you understand. If you are not certain, ask. You might use your child's own words, but rephrase them in the form of a question. Or you could comment on the implied content or feelings of the child's message:

> Child: "I hate that stupid Richy. He makes me feel so dumb."
> Parent: "It sounds as if he really hurts your feelings."

Responding in this way is like being a mirror. Your response reflects the attitudes and feelings that you hear, giving the child the chance to say, "Yes, that's it" or "No, what I mean is . . " and so forth. Reflective listening is one of the best ways to encourage your children to talk to you. It helps children feel respected, understood, and better able to identify the sources of their emotions or problems.

Just as there are "conversation invitations," there are "conversation-stoppers." Here are a few: "Oh, just forget about it," or "Tomorrow's another day," or "You shouldn't feel that way." Although you may be fully intending to help your child feel better, such phrases often stop the conversation by denying the depth of the child's feelings. Children may feel as if their worries are unimportant and may decide that their parents don't understand or aren't interested.

Another conversation-stopper is blame or criticism. When parents respond to a child's conversation by saying, "That's ridiculous!" or "Wherever did you get that crazy idea?", the child will feel inferior and inadequate. This negative criticism hurts and is a strong incentive to your child to keep things to himself or herself. So be sure to use "conversation invitations" to keep those lines open!

Of course parents don't always have to be on the listening end of a conversation. We can express our own thoughts and our feelings to our children in appropriate measures. By saying, "I've got this problem. Maybe you can help me figure out a solution," you are teaching your children the value of talking things out. It also gives children the opportunity to practice good listening skills as they respond to us. This does not mean that we should burden young children with adult worries or expect them to have the wisdom and understanding that only maturity can bring. But we can be open, honest, and human, and we can gain from the insight and care of our children.

Perhaps the most important thing that parents can do is to remember that each child is a gift and a trust—not a possession. We are responsible for loving our children, for giving them our highest respect, and for making clear our values. But we do not own them. Our sons and daughters are entrusted to us. With the gift of children God provides us with the opportunity to help shape and to be shaped by them. Instead of wanting to limit our children, we can give them some of the greatest gifts possible: the freedom to feel, to think, to inquire, and to choose.

THE STORY OF HANNAH

The story of Hannah found in 1 Samuel is an example of one mother who was able to be this kind of parent. Hannah longed for a child. She acknowledged to herself, to her husband, and even to Eli the priest that she felt empty, hurt, bitter, and sad. She spent time in prayer, telling God her dreams and her sorrows. When at last little Samuel was born, Hannah realized that this child was a gift from God. She was thrilled to have his life entrusted to her and did everything that modern authorities say a nurturing mother should do: she cuddled Samuel, held him close to nurse, surrounded him with her love. But Hannah knew that she had no right to own, keep, or limit her son. She knew that his relationship with God came first.

It must have been difficult for Hannah to take Samuel to live at the Temple, but that is what she did. She carefully passed on to him the necessary skills to be self-assured and competent. She trusted his ability to think for himself. She taught him to be faithful to God and to care about right living. She took care of his physical needs, lovingly sewing his new clothes, and then she stepped back and let him go.

A PRAYER OF HOPE AND EXPECTATION

Loving God,

We come to you as expectant parents, filled with hopes and dreams for our children. We want them to be happy and fulfilled, to have strong self-images and a respect and appreciation for their bodies. We want them to know how to give and to receive love.

Help us not to limit our children, but to be aware and supportive of their unique identity. Give us the wisdom and courage to pass on our Christian values—not just about sex, but about all of life. Help us to be loving in our families, enabling our children to discover and to experience the beauty of intimate relationships.

And most of all, like Hannah in the Old Testament, let us never forget that children are your gift entrusted to us. Enable us to be faithful to our children and to you.

Amen.

CHAPTER 2

Knowing, Deciding, and Being in Control

DECISION-MAKING SKILLS

When Kathryn was two years old, our friend Mark was pushing her in the swings outside our seminary apartments. Mark, who had no children of his own, was impressed with Kathy's vocabulary and asked her, "What is the biggest word you know?" Kathy thought for a moment and then decided: "House!"

Mark was amused. He expected some long, sophisticated word. We were pleased that our toddler could think, analyze, and make a decision based on her own observations. To Kathy the word *biggest* meant large in size. From her perspective there on the swing, our house was the largest thing she could see.

In preparing to guide our children to make responsible choices about sexuality, one of the most important skills we can teach is the ability to think for themselves. We don't want our children to make impulsive, reckless choices, nor do we want them to act dogmatically, making decisions based on rigid, inflexible positions. We want our sons and daughters to be able to act rationally, identify possibilities, make good choices, and understand consequences. We want their decisions to be based on thoughtful consideration and their actions to reflect such a thoughtfulness. As Proverbs 27:12 says, "The clever see danger and hide; but the simple go on, and suffer for it."

Unfortunately, we sometimes unknowingly stifle independent thinking during the child's early years. We decide what clothes our children will wear, how they will use their free time, and how to spend their allowance. We sometimes make our child feel that his or her opinions and wishes are wrong or unimportant. We can sometimes be quick to find fault and to criticize, or become our child's on-call problem-solver. We stand ready to take over the completion of projects when our child asks for help. While our energies would be better invested in teaching conflict resolution skills to our children, we're often tempted to function as a referee in our children's disagreements. We parents impose value judgments, deny discussion, and sometimes make little effort to consider the validity of the child's point of view. How easy to say, "Don't argue with me. When you've lived as long as I have, maybe you'll understand. For now, you'll do what I say."

It's not that we parents are unloving. Maybe we're just trying to say, "I don't want you to have to go through the painful experiences I've had. I want the best for you, and I truly believe that this way is the best." But insisting that children conform to parents' beliefs and authority can backfire. Children can end up feeling powerless and alienated, depending on parents to come to their rescue. Their desire and ability to think for themselves may never grow.

Giving children facts is not enough to help them make sound decisions. Management experts who consult with large businesses agree that the decision-making process is a cycle. All decisions, whether complex or simple, involve these steps:

- *identifying the problem or challenge.*
- *investigating the relevant facts and alternatives.*
- *analyzing the potential consequences.*
- *choosing and implementing an action.*
- *evaluating the result to see if you have addressed the original problem.*

Information gathering is only a part of this, not the conclusion. It is one thing to have the necessary information and quite another to decide how we are going to act upon that information. Our knowledge is influenced by our attitudes, our desires, and our values.

Our role as parents is to assist our children in being able to recognize potential problems or issues. We want to make sure that they learn how and where to look for relevant information and how to evaluate its meaning. We want them to form sound decisions and to act upon those decisions with certainty.

We will probably not be there when our daughters are faced with the argument, "If you love me, you'll let me." We cannot follow our son everywhere to urge him to practice self-control. We will not be the ones to decide if our children are ready to handle the consequences of sexual involvement. These are personal decisions that must be made by individuals. Parents can influence the outcome, but they must do it early by cultivating decision-making competence in their sons and daughters.

IDEAS FOR HELPING CHILDREN TO THINK

Here are some things parents can do to help children learn to think for themselves. We can encourage our children to be observant. As we read a picture book together, we can say, "Can you name everything you see on this page?" As we go for a walk, we can stop to watch an ant and guess what plans it has for the bread crumb it carries. We can lie on the grass with our eyes closed and attempt to identify all of the sounds we hear. Neglecting to be alert, we fail to notice so much of life. When we are making decisions, we cannot afford to miss important data. It pays to pay attention!

Children can learn to be aware of what is happening in their environment. They can also learn to check on the accuracy of what they observe. Are things really as they appear to be? Did others see the same thing, or something different? What happens if you look at it from a different angle?

A fun way to help your family practice this kind of thinking is by playing object games. Select a variety of objects (almost anything will do) and place them on the table. Ask your children to observe the items carefully for a few minutes, noting as many details as they can. Then remove or cover the objects and take turns asking questions to see how observant each person was: "How many buttons were on the bear's shirt? What color was the pencil?" A second object game is to place a selection of objects on the table and again ask your family to observe them carefully. Then, while the children cover their eyes, remove several of the items and change the position of a few of the remaining ones. Then ask your family to open their eyes and identify what is different. A third game is to place objects in a large grocery bag and challenge your children to identify the objects by touch. Ask them to describe the items by their physical characteristics: "Is it rough? Is it hard? Does it feel like it is made of plastic?" These games encourage children to use their senses, to make distinctions, and to give careful thought to their decisions.

Another way to teach your children to think independently is to ask them to make comparisons—to see similarities and differences and to identify the relationship of one thing or activity to another: "How is the family on your favorite TV show like our family? How is it different? Would you like to be more like them, or should they be more like us? How are older children different from younger children? In what ways are the boys in your class different from the girls? In what ways are they the same?"

We can also encourage thinking by asking our children why they believe something has occurred, or what they think might be a possible solution to a problem. For example, when a lamp gets broken, parents might sit their children down and ask: "How do you think this happened? How can we keep it from happening again?" This is a more productive alternative to angrily scolding, "I've told you a thousand times not to play baseball in the living room!" This kind of thinking helps your children to see that there are consequences to actions and that they often have the power to affect those consequences by their decisions. They also learn that they have the power to make different choices with different outcomes in the future. When your children are fighting over fast-food restaurants, you can say, "Maybe it would be better if Daddy chose tonight" or "Perhaps we should each take turns in choosing," instead of saying, "That's it! We're never eating out again!" You might propose possible solutions, helping children to see alternatives and building their relational skills.

As we guide our children in learning to make decisions, we must allow them the right to analyze, evaluate, and speak honestly. Parents are understandably afraid of this. It hurts when a child says, "Mom, that dress makes you look fat," and we tend to lash out with some statement about how children should treat their parents with respect. Children should respect their parents, and they have no right to say mean and hurtful things. But making critical judgments is a part of the thinking process. It is a step in assigning worth or determining value. Criticizing seems to come easily; stating the reasoning behind our evaluation is more difficult. A more productive response might be, "Why does it make me look fat? Is it the color, or the design? Is it too small?" We need to teach our children to use the word *because*. Show them how important it is to have a valid reason behind their opinions, so evaluating does not degenerate into indiscriminate faultfinding.

DISCOVERING AND CLAIMING VALUES

Values are the anchors of our behavior. Without values, we would drift with every whim and temptation. Every decision we make is either based upon a value or is helping to shape new values. If we know what we value, we can begin to consciously organize our lives around that system.

If only it were that easy! Often our values are in conflict. "How can I know what is good? I don't know how I feel about that issue. What criteria do I use to make a particular decision?" Tough questions for adults. Imagine how difficult it must be for children! However, helping children form values is one of the most important and exciting tasks of parenthood. This does not mean that parents simply imprint all of their own likes and dislikes onto their children, but they can help their sons and daughters choose, recognize, and claim personal values for themselves.

Young children have values, even when they are not able to state them. They value security and so prefer to stay close to their mother. They may refuse to sit in a high chair because they value being part of the family and want to sit on a regular chair at the table like everyone else. Older children can begin to identify their values. Parents can help in this process by frequently asking them, "Would you like to do this?" or "What do you think about that?" Some sample questions parents might use to encourage children to consider their values could be:

- *Would you like to buy an ice cream cone or save your money for a toy?*
- *Would you rather be a great athlete, a great scientist, or a famous comedian?*
- *Would you rather go to the beach or to the amusement park?*
- *Do you want to get married?*
- *What makes you angry?*
- *If someone gave you ten million dollars, what would you do with it?*
- *What is the best book you've read this month?*
- *What has been the happiest moment in your life?*
- *If you could invite some television characters to your birthday party, whom would you invite?*
- *What is the worst day of the week for you?*

22

These kinds of questions encourage children to consider and identify what is important and meaningful in their lives. Parents who listen carefully to the answers will be able to help their children note what values are demonstrated. Together parents and children can set goals and make choices based on those values—choices that we hope will provide deep and lasting satisfaction. We are not suggesting that parents should grill their children with questions. These can be lighthearted discussion topics for the supper table. In fact sociologists have found that around the supper table is where parents most often talk about their own values!

It is only normal that we should want our children to share many of our values. But before children decide whether they wish to claim these values for themselves, they must understand the meaning of these values for their own lives. Parents shouldn't assume that children are clear about parents' values. We owe it to our children to talk about the things we stand for, explain why we believe as we do, and demonstrate how we live out those beliefs in our daily lives.

For example, churchgoing parents may assume that their daughters and sons know that kindness is a Christian value, then become upset when their youngsters are selfish or mean. Explaining why they value loving actions helps children connect parental values and expectations. Demonstrating kindness is perhaps the most important way to teach its importance. Parents who thank their children for acts of kindness reinforce its value. Sharing relevant passages from the Bible (such as 1 Corinthians 13) stresses the value of loving actions and teaches children that your values are based on a higher authority.

Parents may mistakenly assume that in not talking about premarital intercourse, they are communicating to their children that they believe such behavior is wrong. In fact, the children might be getting the message that sex is an "unmentionable" topic. Parents may then become angry, hurt, ashamed, and confused when their teenager becomes pregnant. Parents need to clearly communicate their actual beliefs to their children and explain why they feel strongly about the issue. They need to explain that premarital intercourse goes against their moral code and violates their religious beliefs. Parents should feel free to talk about their own teen years, about the joyful experiences they had in high school, and about how sad it would have been to miss out on those memories because of an unplanned baby. They can discuss how difficult it is to support a family and explain the reasons why many people choose to earn a degree or be settled in a job before having a child. Parents can talk about how many single, unwed mothers live in poverty right here in the United States. Parents can talk about their belief that every child deserves enough food to eat, a warm place to sleep, and the love of two parents.

With this kind of communication, parents are sharing an important part of themselves with their child. They are holding up a value and offering it as a good choice for their child. They are not forcing the value upon their son or daughter, but are enabling him or her to see and understand the validity of that opinion.

HOW DO YOU TEACH SELF-CONTROL?

Most parents want their children to be self-disciplined. We want to raise daughters and sons who are capable of directing and controlling their own behavior—not just so that they will "stay out of trouble," but so that they will direct their energies toward paths that lead to personal happiness and success.

How can parents help teach self-control? If parents pressure a child to behave in a certain way, the control is coming from the outside, not from within the child. Such a child may say, "I'd do it if I could, but my mean Mom won't let me! I wish I were grown up, so I could do what I please!" At the same time, if adults never put outside restraints on a child, it is unlikely that an inner discipline will develop to keep that child from being unruly and out of control. Proverbs 25:28 says, "Like a city breached, without walls, is one who lacks self-control."

Children need some boundaries to prevent them from harming themselves and others. Surveys show that most accidents that happen in the home and that involve children occur in the late afternoon when parents are tired and preoccupied with preparing supper. Other recent studies indicate that people who are allowed to be bullies as children grow up to be adult bullies. Being given the freedom to do whatever one wants does not usually result in self-control! Self-discipline, then, is not an inherent trait—it must be learned.

The first steps in helping children to learn self-control should begin when children are young. Build their self-esteem so that they are strong and resilient. Help children to respect themselves. Then communicate to them your values and ethics, providing them with a basis for forming their own goals and expectations for behavior. Teach them to think and to make decisions. Give them opportunities to make choices. Be available to listen and assist as they work through those choices.

Next, expect your children to take responsibility for their actions. Let them know that when you say "No," it is for a good reason and that you mean what you say. Don't always bail them out of predicaments or try to cover up their mistakes. Teach them that there are natural or expected consequences to some actions and that we have to live with those consequences.

Another important element in teaching about self-control is making sure that we model self-control in our actions. Children copy behaviors! In our home, for example, the children know that neither mother nor father places a high value on having an uncluttered environment. When we're involved in an exciting project, perfect order is not on our priority list. It is little wonder, then, that when we decide to clean house, our kids protest and complain! They have not learned self-discipline with regards to always keeping their rooms clean because their parents are undisciplined in this area.

Timmy and Kathy do see us going to the library to do research. They observe the hours we spend planning and preparing for sermons or workshops. They watch us go over a manuscript word by word, editing and rewriting. They see how much we love to read. As a result we are not surprised that they take responsibility to get their homework done without our prodding. Seeing Mom practicing the piano every day, our children take for granted that they will practice too. It becomes part of our daily routine and our self-discipline.

If we want our children to exercise self-control in eating habits, drug use, or sexual activity, we should model that same discipline ourselves. The success rate of such modeling has been verified by a Swedish study. The study showed that when parents told their children to exhibit self-discipline, but did not model that self-control themselves, their instructions were ineffective. But when parents were well-disciplined in an area, their children showed high rates of self-control in that same area. This took place despite the fact that these parents seldom spoke about the need for discipline with their children.

As parents model self-control, as they provide the external discipline that they hope will be internalized, and as they talk with their children about self-discipline, they are helping the child to develop a conscience. The process cannot be forced. We help our children by setting clear goals and expectations, by rewarding positive behavior, and by praising their efforts and successes. Strict parental rules and harsh punishment tend to be ineffective methods for enhancing self-control. They are more likely to produce resentment and hostility than integrity and conscience.

One of the biblical accounts that best exemplifies self-control is the story of Paul and Silas and the earthquake. Arrested, beaten, and humiliated for the "crime" of casting out an evil spirit, the two men found themselves locked and chained in prison. About midnight, while they were singing hymns of praise and praying to God, a great earthquake struck the prison. The earthquake opened the doors, loosened their chains, and Paul and Silas were free.

Paul and Silas might have interpreted the broken chains and open doors as God's signal to escape.

However, they realized that for them to leave the prison would most certainly have caused their jailer to lose his job or even his life. In a remarkable show of self-control they remained where they were. When the jailer returned, expecting to find his prisoners gone, he was astonished to find them still there. He so admired their courage and inner strength that he asked how he might become more like them. The example of self-control demonstrated by Paul and Silas led to the baptism of the jailer and his entire family.

While we trust that our sons and daughters will never have to face beatings and prison as did Silas and Paul, we know that they will face other threats. They will need to make many choices—choices that will require strong inner values and self-control.

LEARNING HOW TO SAY "NO"

When parents hear the statistics for teenage drug abuse, alcoholism, and pregnancy, they become frightened—and rightfully so. They know that their sons and daughters are being pressured to experiment with alcohol, drugs, and sex; and parents wonder, "Will they be able to say 'No'?" Parents of younger children hear stories about child molesters and worry: "Will my children realize that they have the right to tell an adult: 'Don't touch me'?"

A necessary part of good parenting is teaching our children to be assertive. Assertive behavior means acting in ways to preserve one's dignity and self-respect. Our children need to have faith in themselves and need to know that they can stand up for their rights. We must assure them that friends and family members do not always have to agree, that strong relationships can survive disagreements, and that they have the right to say "No" without giving excuses or justifying their reasons!

Many children don't realize that people can, and will, attempt to use emotional manipulation on them. Young children are taught to respect their parents and other adults and are scolded when they don't obey. They are trained to be obedient and polite and are accustomed to letting others decide how they will act, think, or feel. Boys and girls can be intimidated by another person's apparent logic and may feel foolish or disrespectful if they don't go along with that person's desires.

There will be occasions when children of all ages will need to stand up for themselves, either to protect their rights or their bodies. We are giving our children a good gift when we tell them, "You can make your own decisions and stick to them—even when your friends are pushing you to change your mind. I trust your judgment, and you should too." Children can be taught to be persistent. They can learn how to remain firm in their position without becoming angry or hostile and without feeling anxious and guilty.

An excellent book on assertiveness that we recommend is *Yes, I Can Say No—A Parent's Guide to Assertiveness Training for Children*, by Manuel J. Smith (Arbor House, 1986). (This resource is out of print, but may be available in your church or community library.) In this book Smith outlines "Assertive Rights" that both adults and children have: the right to be your own judge and to be responsible for your thoughts, feelings, and actions; the right to act without making excuses for your behavior and saying, "It's not my fault"; the right to change your mind and to admit making a mistake or to say, "I don't know"; the right to choose your friends; the right to make a decision without having to prove its logic; the right to say, "I don't understand"; the right to be less than perfect and still feel okay about yourself. Smith's book contains ninety-four sample dialogues that show how children can give assertive responses to real-life situations. Families can read these dialogues to hear what assertive answers sound like and can roleplay similar situations to practice making their own assertive responses.

DAVID AND BATHSHEBA SHOULD HAVE SAID "NO"

As Bible stories so often point out, adults do not always act as they should. King David, for example, made some poor decisions with regards to sex. He spied on Bathsheba while she was bathing. Drawn to her beauty, David allowed his desire to control his actions and sought a way to get around the fact that she was already married. What happened to David's self-control? Why was he not able to say "No" to his desires? Did he never learn self-discipline? What was his understanding of sexual responsibility?

What about Bathsheba? Did she feel she had no right or power to say "No" to David's intentions? Could she have been assertive? Would it have been possible for her to refuse David's wishes?

When Bathsheba became pregnant with David's child, David arranged to have her husband Uriah come home from battle for the night, hoping to make it appear that the child was Uriah's. But the plan did not work, and David finally resorted to having Uriah sent to the front lines, where he was killed.

David's actions had an effect on himself, on his nation, and on his family. The child conceived by David and Bathsheba died shortly after birth, leaving David feeling depressed and guilty. How different the story might have ended if David had thought through the possible consequences of his actions and said, "With God's help, I will say no." How differently the story might have ended if women of that day had been raised to think of themselves as equals and not possessions to be used. How much better our own lives and the lives of our children will be when we too can be assertive and comfortable with the word *no*.

A PRAYER FOR CLARITY OF THOUGHT

Loving God,

Help us to raise thoughtful children—not just thoughtful in terms of being caring and kind, but as persons who are able to think.

Free us from wanting to keep our children overly dependent on us. Help us to enable our sons and daughters to make wise decisions and choices and to have the ability to carry out the actions they decide upon.

Help us to communicate our values and our love for you, to practice self-control in our own lives, and to be assertive in our "Yes" and in our "No."

Amen.

CHAPTER 3

Understanding Our Children's Sexuality

BECOMING AWARE OF OUR SEXUALITY

Can you remember when you first realized that you were a boy or a girl? Most adults cannot. As infants we neither knew nor cared about such differences—even though people made a fuss over what a beautiful girl or a strong and husky boy we were.

Over the next two years we began to notice that boys and girls dressed differently, and we observed that our mother and father did not have identical hairstyles. We might have observed that our brother or sister did not urinate in the same way we did. By the time we were two and a half or three years old, we were able to say with certainty, "No, I am not a girl" or "No, I am not a boy." We were able to identify our own gender and the gender of others with reasonable accuracy.

The process by which children become aware of their sexuality is a gradual one, occurring in predictable stages. This does not mean that infants are asexual or without sexuality. Every person, regardless of age, is a sexual being from the moment of birth. Sexuality is an integral part of every person's identity.

Some adults feel uncomfortable with the idea that children are sexual beings. "How can someone this innocent and pure be called sexual?" They don't want children to demonstrate sexual behaviors or knowledge. Observing children engaging in an activity that an adult sees as sexual can cause the adult to feel concern.

We are not suggesting that parents should simply ignore or laugh off a child's inappropriate sexual behaviors. It is a parent's responsibility to help children form strong values and to communicate the difference between appropriate and inappropriate behavior. As adults we have learned much about life and relationships. We know that issues of sexuality hold the potential for both joy and pain, and we feel an obligation to make sure our children are aware of possible danger areas. In keeping with the wisdom of the psalmist,

> *Things we have heard and known,*
> *that our ancestors have told us.*
> *We will not hide them from their children.*
> Psalm 78:3-4a

Sometimes a child's innocent and natural actions can be perceived by adult standards to appear inappropriate or suggestive. Normally we discourage those behaviors and suggest more acceptable behaviors. At the same time we unknowingly encourage children to act in even more suggestive ways by rationalizing that she will look so cute or that he will look all grown up. It isn't easy to know how to communicate a healthy attitude toward a child's sexuality.

When our daughter Kathryn was in kindergarten, she participated in a dancing and gymnastics class. For the spring recital each little girl was expected to purchase two sequined outfits. The day of the recital these five- and six-year-olds spent the entire afternoon rolling their hair in electric rollers and cementing the curls on the top of their heads with hair spray and hundreds of bobby pins. The makeup crew sculpted the girls' faces with blush, eye shadow, mascara, and lipstick. When nervous tears made the makeup run, more was liberally applied to hide the evidence. At the close of the show, everyone said what beautiful young ladies they were! No one said, "My, how sexy you looked," but that was the implied message.

The following afternoon several of these little dancers were taken to the park to play. It was a hot, humid Texas day, and most of the girls were wearing short sundresses. One small girl, praised on the previous evening for looking so appealing, began to turn cartwheels and stand on her head, giving full view of her underpants. Her mother, dressed in short shorts and a halter top, rushed over to give her daughter a swat on her behind. "Nice little girls don't show their underwear!" she scolded. "Especially with boys around!" Imagine the little girl's confusion!

There is nothing inherently wrong with wanting our daughters to be feminine. Some five- and six-year-old girls may already have a desire to look pretty. For such girls this desire may be natural. Other equally normal children do not share their interest. However, for prepubescent girls to spend hours "becoming beautiful" is probably not natural or even healthy. On the other hand it is developmentally normal for a small child to try to stand on her head. Little girls at this age don't usually think, "It would be sexy to let a boy see my underwear, so I think I'll turn a cartwheel!" Six-year-olds turn cartwheels for the joy of it.

SEQUENCES OF SEXUAL DEVELOPMENT

Although every person is unique, there appear to be sequences of sexual development that are similar for most children. As children pass through these sequences, it is important for children to be children in all areas of development, including sexual development. As 1 Corinthians 13:11a says: "When I was a child, I spoke like a child, I thought like a child, I reasoned like a child." The passage goes on to say that when we become adults, we put away childish things; but it does not say, "So don't ever act like a child" or "Childhood is not as good as adulthood" or "Children should behave as miniature adults." Each step of development represents a stage that should be affirmed as a part of God's creative plan. Our appreciation can echo the words of the psalmist:

> For it was you who formed my inward parts;
>   you knit me together in my mother's womb.
> I praise you, for I am fearfully and wonderfully made.
>   Psalm 139:13-14a

At every age level there are ways in which boys and girls tend to differ, as well as ways they are alike. While some of these similarities and differences may be biological in origin, others are cultural. Frequently the line between the two is blurry. Research findings in the area of developmental differences have often been challenged by conflicting data.

The information that follows details sexual development and ways parents can be supportive throughout all five age levels.

Before Birth

STAGES IN SEXUAL DEVELOPMENT

Sexual development begins at the moment of fertilization, when the father's sperm contributes either an X or Y chromosome to pair with the X chromosome of the mother's ovum. The cells of boys and girls are slightly different. The male cell contains an X chromosome and a smaller Y chromosome (XY), while the female cell contains two large X chromosomes (XX).

John Money of Johns Hopkins University is one of many authorities who believe that both maternal and fetal hormones also affect the development of body gender.[1] Hormones—biochemical substances that are present in the blood in minute amounts—determine the kind of external sex organs an embryo will develop. Up until about the sixth week after conception, or possibly as late as the twelfth week for females, the tissue structures that will become the female or male reproductive organs are the same. Unless male hormones are present, a female body is formed. Hormones, then, appear to be responsible for the visible differences between females and males.

Other prenatal chemical adjustments are also believed to have an effect on the sex of a fetus. For example, barbiturates taken by pregnant women have been found to prevent the male sex organs from developing properly.

Sexual identity is not established at conception, nor is it determined during the months in the womb. Hundreds of factors in a person's childhood environment will help to shape his or her personality. However, the prenatal months have a great influence as the genetic blueprint is laid down and then as hormonal activity occurs. These will serve as the foundation for later physical, mental, and sexual development.

PROVIDING A SOLID BASIS FOR CHILDREN'S SEXUALITY

Expectant parents who want to provide a solid basis for their child's sexuality start by obtaining good prenatal care and by avoiding the use of drugs, alcohol, and tobacco. Medical research has shown that these can be extremely harmful to the fetus. Loving your child, even before birth, increases the possibility of that child forming a positive self-image in the future. These are the first steps toward a loving relationship.

Birth Through One Year of Age

DIFFERENCES BETWEEN BOYS AND GIRLS

In a study conducted by S.B. Gurvity and K.A. Dodge, a videotape of an infant was shown to mothers and fathers of young babies who were to analyze the child's behavior. The baby was dressed so that viewers could not tell whether it was a boy or a girl.

When the men were told that the baby was a female, they were more likely to say positive things about the infant—characterizing her as gentle, less aggressive, sweet, a soft crier, and sociable. When the men were told that this same baby was a boy, they tended to describe the baby as fussy, irritable, and aggressive. The women, on the other hand, were more likely to respond positively to the baby when told it was a boy. They would assign to the child traditional masculine attributes, describing the baby as strong, active, and independent. The women would characterize this same infant less favorably when told it was a girl. Many of these impressions of maleness and femaleness are qualities we see when we look for them, rather than being actual distinctions. At the same time, some sex-related differences do exist between baby boys and girls—many of which are either proven or well-supported by most published studies.

34

First of all, according to U.S. census figures, more males are conceived than females, with approximately 105 boys born in the United States for every 100 girls. But the percentage of miscarriages and the infant mortality rate are higher for males than for females. The death rate within the first month after birth is nearly 25 percent higher for males than for females. Boys are more susceptible to hereditary disorders, disease, and malnutrition at all ages, and the disproportionate ratio of male to female deaths continues throughout life.

At birth boys are heavier than girls, with larger heads and faces, more muscle, and less fat. Baby girls are physically more mature than boys. They learn to walk earlier and tend to cut teeth sooner. Girls are more sensitive to touch, pain, cold, and taste than boys are. Some studies show that boys startle more easily than girls, cry more frequently, and are more difficult to soothe. Infant boys and girls also have different sleep patterns.

The right side of the brain, which is considered responsible for processing language, develops earlier in females than in males. Girls, then, frequently talk earlier and excel in verbal activities. Some studies have indicated that infant girls can recognize faces at an earlier age than infant boys. By six months of age girls show an interest in smiling before boys do and are more easily encouraged to smile.

STAGES IN SEXUAL DEVELOPMENT

Both male and female infants show evidence of sexual response. Infant boys have erections—often during a diaper change. Males experience erections prior to birth and are sometimes born with an erection. Females, prior to birth and as infants, experience vaginal lubrication and orgasmic responses.

As infants gain command of their muscles, they begin to move their arms and reach out for things. At approximately sixteen weeks babies' hands are at their mouths. At twenty weeks they move their hands and arms in the area of the chest. By the fortieth week they are beginning to explore in the area of the thighs and genitals. As babies make significant advances of their self-discovery, they play with the navel and touch the penis or vulva. In some ways the baby's own body is just one of the many things that infants grasp and manipulate. But babies also discover that touching their genitals results in a pleasurable sensation, which may be the onset of masturbation. Early in life both sexes experience feelings that are directly related to their being female or male.

Actions such as making eye contact (at four weeks), smiling at the sight of a mother's face (at eight weeks), crying when someone leaves (at twenty weeks), or withdrawing from strangers (at 32 weeks) all show how babies are beginning the process of relating to others. This has sexual implications, because establishing an intimate relationship with another person is part of what sexuality is all about.

One of the major ways that infants respond to and communicate with others is through the sense of touch. Babies feel warmth and affection when Daddy plays with them. They usually like to be cuddled. When babies nurse, they not only experience physical pleasure, but are also nourished by the security and comfort of their mother's body. They sense nervousness or fear by the way they are held, and are aware of the holder's emotional state. Babies' cries are pleas for comfort. They welcome being picked up, rubbed gently on the tummy or the back, or rocked to sleep. Such quiet touches are calming and help children to initiate control on their own.

Seventy-five years ago childhood authorities encouraged parents to avoid spoiling their babies with too much handling. Parents were told to let babies cry, to feed them on an exact schedule, and to avoid overusing the rocking chair or cradle. Babies, parents were told, should not be smothered with touch. Today we know that physical touch is essential in order for a baby to thrive. Touch influences learning, growth rates, sociability, the ability to withstand stress, and even immunological development. Infants who are not touched experience setbacks in growth. They may have speech defects, mental retardation, decreased height and weight, and are sometimes said to have "psychosocial dwarfism." Persons who are not held and fondled may suffer later in life from either an extreme hunger for body contact or an intense repulsion to touch. Researchers Mary Ainsworth et al.[2] and M. Louise Biggar[3] have also found that infants who are physically rejected by their mothers in the first three months of life will show unusually high degrees of anger by the time they are a year old.

It has been found that massaging babies' backs may help them build a healthy body image and improve their neurological development. Holding and touching infants helps them to stay healthy, increases their skin's sensitivity to stimulus, and enhances their socialization skills. Dr. Anneliese F. Korner[4] has discovered that picking up crying newborn babies and holding them close to the shoulder almost invariably causes the infant to become bright-eyed and alert. Babies who are alert have more opportunities to relate to the people and the environment that they see. When a baby is only soothed and not lifted to the shoulder, there is no significant increase in visual alertness. Early contact—touching an infant within thirty minutes after birth—results in significantly stronger bonding attachments between parent and child. These early-held children cry less and smile and laugh more than babies who are not cuddled immediately after birth.

Touch, then, is an essential ingredient in a small child's sexual development. It encompasses and enhances so many areas of that sexuality—the ability to relate intimately with another person and to be sensitive to their needs and emotions; the ability to experience pleasurable sensations and to feel good about one's own body; and the ability to accept, appreciate, and reciprocate physical and emotional tenderness from special individuals.

Psychologist Erik Erikson[5] suggests that during the first year of life, babies are learning to trust themselves and others. This too has an impact on children's experience of sexuality. When babies feel safe and confident, they become free to reach out past themselves and to feel secure in accepting the love of others. Trust enables persons to disclose themselves to someone they love—an important step on the way to becoming vulnerable and open in relationships.

PROVIDING A SOLID BASIS FOR CHILDREN'S SEXUALITY

We parents can help our newborn children develop a positive sexuality by helping them thrive. We can give our tiny sons every chance to survive that statistically difficult first month. We can provide good medical care and proper nutrition. Mothers can choose to breastfeed their babies, knowing that human milk provides the best nutrition possible for the child. Breast milk is more easily digested than cow's milk.

The colostrum in the mother's milk provides antibodies that protect the baby against disease. Breastfeeding is also an ideal opportunity for the mother-child closeness that is so critical to early bonding. In instances where breastfeeding is either not possible or not desired, parents should still hold and cuddle their babies during feedings and at other times.

It is natural for parents to become frustrated and overwhelmed at times—especially when they are exhausted. Remember that many little girls dislike being cold, and many little boys cry a lot. Our children are not trying to upset us. They are simply trying to communicate through the only tool they have. If we respond to children with anger and irritation, they will sense it, even if they do not yet understand our feelings. Treating tiny children as if they are doing something wrong when they really can't help how they are acting may lead to a negative self-image later in life.

Remember the importance of loving, warm, gentle touches. We can cuddle our babies, massage their backs, make eye contact as we talk to them. Instead of always leaving them in a crib or infant seat, we can hold them upright on our shoulder and let them see the world. When our babies begin to discover different parts of their bodies, we should not slap their hands because of our own discomfort or embarrassment. The way we hold and touch our children can assure them that we are persons they can trust. Building trust in our children will help them later to form the intimate bonds and ties that will make other relationships possible.

One and Two Years of Age

DIFFERENCES BETWEEN BOYS AND GIRLS

During the next two years of life, differences between girls and boys become evident. Boys display more anger than girls, even by as early as seven months of age, and the differences are often sizable by the age of two or two and a half. Many boys engage in highly rough-and-tumble play, and although girls frequently do so in moderate ways, research suggests that about 20 percent of boys are much rougher than the girls.

Difference in play style shows itself in the use of toys. Boys appear to play with trucks and cars more than girls, even though small children are much more likely to see their mothers driving the family car. Parents may offer children identical toys, yet find that boys and girls choose and play with those toys in dissimilar ways. A study in modern Israel found that most parents gave dolls to their toddlers. While the girls tended to play with their dolls as imitation babies, the boys might jump on the dolls or pound with them as if they were hammers. Surprisingly, evidence does not show that little boys are encouraged to be more aggressive than little girls. Parents and nursery workers appear to be more aware of boys' aggression and quicker to discourage it, while they tend to ignore the aggressive behavior of girls. Some researchers believe that the source of male aggression is hormonal. Studies have found that hormonal treatments can make female animals behave as aggressively as males. Researchers Carol Jacklin and Eleanor Maccoby[6] of Stanford University believe that boys are genetically more prepared to become aggressive—not inherently aggressive, but requiring only small amounts of stimulation to bring out aggression.

Another sex-related difference observed in toddlers is the degree of cooperation. In an experiment by L. Shapio[7] at Harvard University, previously unacquainted two-year-olds were brought together in pairs. When a single toy was placed between the children, the pairs of boys would treat one another suspiciously, evaluate each other's posture and facial expression, then fight over possession of the toy. The pairs of girls appeared to be more trusting of each other playing together cooperatively.

Females, as a group, learn to talk earlier than males. Girls have a larger vocabulary and use grammar and pronunciation more correctly. By two years of age girls usually know the names of their family and friends. Boys, as a rule, do not. Parents of a two-year-old daughter may believe that their little girl is smarter than the neighbor's little boy. Parents of boys can be assured that their sons will soon begin to exhibit their own unique strengths.

STAGES IN SEXUAL DEVELOPMENT

The sexuality of one- and two-year-old children is being shaped by greater physical skills, emerging independence, increasing self-aware-ness, social learning, and the beginning of friendship. The psychologist Erikson refers to this as the stage of autonomy or self-determination. Toddlers are no longer dependent on close contact with mother, but want to walk and run, to explore and manipulate the world. When mother makes suggestions and demands, the average 21-month-old obeys only about half of the time. Children of this age are becoming aware of their own wants and are building their self-esteem and self-identity. Parents' punishments may cause feelings of shame and doubt.

Toddlers are beginning to want companionship. These companions are often family members—parents, brothers, and sisters. Sometimes ones and twos will actively play with another person, but they may be satis-fied simply to have another person close by.

One- and two-year-olds are interested in the human body. By age two many toddlers recognize photographs of themselves as well as their own image in a mirror. By two and a half, children refer to themselves as "I" and to others as "you." They begin to notice differences between the sexes—differences in bodies and differences in the ways those bodies are dressed. At this age children state their sex negatively—"I am not a boy" or "I am not a girl." They watch curiously when others are undressed. They are conscious of their genitals and may handle them.

One- and two-year-olds learn about life by observing and by imitating. Children watch, compare, and copy behaviors—especially the actions of their parents—and adopt behaviors that produce rewards. With this process children begin to learn skills and attitudes that are essential for living in society. Pressures are put upon children to do things in a gender-appropriate way, starting with the play materials that are offered to them and the clothes in which they are dressed.

One of the major tasks of a toddler is to begin toilet training. Parents' attitudes toward this training will probably affect the child's feelings about sex, simply because the same body parts are involved. Taught that it is dirty to urinate or to have a bowel movement, they may conclude that sex also is dirty. If children receive criticism about their lack of control, they may feel tension or shame in relation to these body parts. Parents who are uncomfortable using the correct names of body parts during toilet training often have difficulty talking openly and candidly about sex when the child is older.

PROVIDING A SOLID BASIS FOR CHILDREN'S SEXUALITY

Parents of toddlers can build a solid basis for their children's sexuality by providing a variety of toys for both sexes. Parents must then be willing to accept children's choices of toys and how the children choose to enjoy the toys—even when their choices are not consistent with traditional images of little-girl or little-boy behaviors.

We should probably not expect a rough-and-tumble boy to be quiet and subdued all the time. We can give him a doll or a bear to cuddle, but we do not want to make him feel that it is bad to be active. When our son is behaving in ways that we feel are too aggressive, however, we don't ignore it. If he wants to pound and starts to use a doll as the hammer, we can give him the proper toys. This does not mean we take away the doll. We talk about how babies need love and like to be held and hugged and how hammers are for pounding and for building. We give little boys an opportunity to use their muscles and still let them know that hurting people is not something we do, even in fun or imaginary play.

We train children in positive sexuality by teaching cooperation. Sharing is a difficult concept for a child to learn. Yet a truly intimate relationship with another person is impossible without sharing yourself. We need to teach our sons and daughters to trust and to expect the best of their companions. The Bible records several stories about sharing. 1 Samuel 18:4 tells how Jonathan gave his own weapons and clothing to David as a sign of friendship. Acts 2:44-45 recalls how early Christians shared everything they owned. The Book of Ruth in the Old Testament tells how Boaz was willing to share his crops with Ruth and Naomi. Sharing is indeed a value that we want our children to embrace.

What else can parents do to enhance toddlers' sexuality? We can allow them to have some independence and can provide playmates. We can be as relaxed and unembarrassed about toilet training as we are about eating, sleeping, or any other natural function. We can let toddlers see that their parents care deeply for them and for one another. Husbands and wives can still hold hands when they walk down the beach. Surveys have shown that parents tend not to laugh, smile, or hold hands in public when accompanied by their children. We can change those statistics!

Three Through Five Years of Age

DIFFERENCES BETWEEN BOYS AND GIRLS

Between the age of three and five, a child is in the process of forming his or her sexual identity. During these years his or her gender appears to become fixed, making later changes in sex-role behaviors and attitudes psychologically difficult. Because of this, preschool boys and girls appear to demonstrate many obvious differences, and these differences will probably influence their interests and attitudes for the rest of their lives.

One area of differences is that of play. Although preschool boys and girls still play together, they are beginning to spend more time with children of their own sex and are more likely to fight with a sibling or playmate who is of the opposite sex. Boys tend to play in larger groups than girls do. When given a free choice, boys often choose to play with tricycles, blocks, trucks, cars, and guns. They pretend to be firefighters, airplane pilots, soldiers, or one of their Saturday morning cartoon heroes. A majority of little girls, on the other hand, want to play house with their dolls and pretend to be Mommy. When preschoolers sit down to draw pictures or to tell stories, the little girls include people in their stories and pictures much more frequently than the little boys do. When playing with blocks, boys tend to build towering structures, while girls often prefer enclosing structures.

Preschool boys are slightly heavier and taller than girls of the same age, but girls, on the average, tend to be about six months ahead in general physical, emotional, and social development. Boys' bodies have a higher percentage of muscle and a lower percentage of fat. Their hearts are larger, and their circulatory systems are more efficient. Partly for these reasons boys often can become proficient in throwing a ball and in motor skills requiring coordination of many different muscles. They tend to spend more time than girls do in active outdoor play, excelling in activities that require muscularity and stamina such as climbing, wrestling, and running. Girls usually prefer less strenuous activities, but are better than boys at hopping, skipping, jumping rope, and standing on one foot. Girls also begin to show a superiority in manual dexterity and are better at using scissors and fastening buttons.

As they get older, boys appear to become more adventuresome than girls and to do more exploring. When they have explored near home, boys may want to discover new places. The typical girl stays closer to home. Little boys are more likely to try to pet a strange dog or to climb too high on the playground equipment or to come too close to a deep hole. This may be one reason that they have more accidents than girls do. Researchers believe that girls are not less curious or adventuresome, but are probably subjected to greater restrictions. Parents may be more protective of their daughters and quicker to warn them of possible dangers.

On the other hand, researchers have discovered that even when treated in a similar manner by parents, boys and girls do not always respond in the same way. For example, when parents are authoritative, their daughters appear to increase in independence and their sons appear to be more compliant. It is difficult, then, to determine conclusively why boys and girls act in the ways they do.

STAGES IN SEXUAL DEVELOPMENT

Three-, four-, and five-year-olds are very interested in babies. "Where does a baby come from? Where is it before it is born?" They sometimes believe that a baby is born through the navel. They ask parents to give them a baby brother or sister, and both boys and girls talk about the babies they will have when they grow up.

Preschoolers have a strong interest in the human body—their own and others. They are concerned with their body build and wonder why some children are tall and thin while others are short and plump. They want to know the names of the body organs and want to talk about their awareness of sex. This is the age when boys and girls are full of curiosity about why and how their bodies differ from those of adults and from children of the opposite sex. They want to see their parents' naked bodies. They touch and explore themselves. They ask to look at the bodies of their friends and willingly show theirs in return, examining each other's genitals and watching each other urinate. Such play is natural because it is play, a way in which the child explores the mysterious human body and begins to prepare for adulthood.

Three-, four-, and five-year-olds are aware of their gender and want their appearance to be appropriate for their sex. Little boys sometimes ask to wear ties; little girls like to wear all of their jewelry at once. Choices in hairstyle, clothing, toys, and even colors are made on the basis of being boys and girls. Preschoolers do not appreciate or enjoy being teased about being tomboys or sissies. This is the developmental stage during which children's gender identity is becoming fixed, and children are very aware of sex-role typing. They make strong identifications with the same-sex parent, although they often are not carbon-copies of parental behaviors or attitudes and may even feel jealous over or competitive with that parent.

PROVIDING A SOLID BASIS FOR CHILDREN'S SEXUALITY

Parents of preschoolers are providing sex education as they answer their children's questions about the human body, sex, and babies with honesty and openness. Remember, children are curious about everything. So when our children ask us about where babies come from, we can respond as matter-of-factly as if they had asked why grass is green or where rain comes from. To suddenly become serious, or quiet, or evasive when they ask us about sex sends the message that this subject is somehow different. Our responses to their questions send non-verbal cues.

We can make certain our children have friends of both sexes. If the neighborhood children decide to play doctor, we can remain calm, using it as an opportunity to talk frankly about the human body, rather than condemning such play as evil. We are providing a solid basis for our children's sexuality when we allow them enough choice in the kinds, colors, and textures of clothing they like to wear. This is one way to help them define themselves. We can let our children make choices in other areas too and not demand that they be carbon copies of their parents.

In our family Timothy is a child who cares very deeply about the clothes he wears. He wants to wear suit jackets on Sundays, even though his father would be content to wear blue jeans and a T-shirt every day. Timothy knows what hairstyle he likes and is bothered when he has a "bad hair day." His daddy, on the other hand, rarely thinks about hair and is comfortable with the mussed-up look. As parents, we respect Tim's feelings and wishes concerning his appearance. We know that there are many ways to be masculine, not only his father's way. We want him to be himself and to have good feelings when he looks in the mirror. Positive sexuality, we believe, goes hand in hand with positive self-esteem.

Six Through Eight Years of Age

DIFFERENCES BETWEEN BOYS AND GIRLS

When children reach elementary school age, boys are beginning to assume the general body shape of men, with long, muscular chests and shoulders broader than the hips. Their chests are relatively bigger than girls', and their muscular capacity is about 10 percent greater. Girls are beginning to show feminine distribution of fat, especially around the hips.

First-, second-, and third-grade girls often have best friends, tending to prefer close one-on-one relationships with another girl. Because they play in pairs, they easily cause and experience jealousy, and friendships are not always long-lasting. Boys tend to play in groups and are less exclusive in their relationships. They also appear to be more competitive in some situations and seem to have more enduring friendships than do the girls.

Researchers Whiting and Whiting[8] observed children from around the world in their home settings. They discovered that in almost every culture, girls are more apt than boys to help adults and other children. Boys were more likely to seek attention from adults and attempt to dominate other children, while girls were more pro-social—wanting to help, share, and listen. In another study researchers held a coloring contest for grade school children in which the children had to share crayons for a color-by-number competition. The result of this study also showed that girls were more likely to share, usually handing over a color when asked to. Boys, however, were less likely to share the requested crayon. Furthermore, they were significantly less likely to share with a friend, as opposed to a mere acquaintance, which may indicate that competition is a major factor between friends.

Boys and girls have been found to be fairly equal in reading and vocabulary competence, although girls tend to show faster verbal development.

46

On the average, grade school girls are still ahead of boys in development. More males (such as children who complete a college education) have been identified as child geniuses, and there are more boys than girls who are diagnosed as autistic or hyperactive. Boys also have a much higher percentage of learning disabilities.

STAGES IN SEXUAL DEVELOPMENT

Six-, seven-, and eight-year-old children are still interested in the differences in body structure between boys and girls and may continue to engage in sex play and masturbation. They may begin to fantasize or daydream about sex, but appear to have less interest in sex than they did earlier and ask fewer questions. The questions they do ask begin to be more factual, such as "Does it hurt to have a baby?" At six, children are not self-conscious about their bodies, but by the ages of seven or eight, a sense of sexual modesty may appear. They can become easily embarrassed and tend to desire privacy. They are also learning to respect the rights of others.

School-age children have already formed strong ideas about appropriate sex roles. After about the second grade there seems to be no increase in attachment to sexual stereotypes. Although children may think a bit less stereotypically about what is appropriate for a man or a woman, boys remain under pressure to be masculine. Grade school children tend to segregate themselves by sex on the playground and may start to join boys' or girls' clubs.

Grade school children may delight in off-color jokes or using unacceptable language, even when they may not understand the meaning of what they are repeating. Their attempts to build self-confidence and to establish some independence from adults may explain their behavior, but they are also beginning to form ethical standards of goodness for themselves and for others. They can understand that growing up means assuming more responsibility and accepting consequences for one's decisions. They want approval from parents and peers and are beginning to see that love and respect for others presupposes a love of self.

Early elementary children are interested in the development of babies and will still often request that their parents have one. They can understand the concept that a baby needs both a father and a mother to be formed and that plants and animals each reproduce their own kind. They are able to compare the development of human babies with the development of animals and can learn about life by observing their pets.

PROVIDING A SOLID BASIS FOR CHILDREN'S SEXUALITY

One thing parents can do for their first-, second-, and third-grade children is to encourage them to be pro-social—to form friendships and to act in socially responsible ways. Boys and girls do not automatically know how to work with others or know how to care for the needs and feelings of their friends and family members. They may be selfish or thoughtless—not because they are bad, but because they are immature and because they see their friends acting in these same ways. Children need our support and guidance in these areas, and our praise when they do well. The church and Sunday school can be a major source of this support.

Don remembers an experience he had as a child in which he learned what it means to be pro-social. It was the day of the school picnic. A younger and much smaller boy who had had a difficult year started a fight. Don just stood there while the boy kept hitting him. Don's friends said, "What's the matter with you? Don't let him do that. Hit him back." Don's teachers said, "What a mature thing to do, to just ignore the boy. We are proud of you." What his teachers said made a lasting impression on Don. He is sure that without the positive reinforcement from those adults, the negative reinforcement of his peers would have convinced him to fight back. On that afternoon he learned to care for the needs and feelings of another person—a skill that is essential for the formation of a good sexual relationship.

Parents of elementary children provide a solid foundation for their children's sexuality when they help their children become thoughtful and caring. They help their daughters and sons become well-adjusted in their sexual identity when they determine not to put their children under undue academic pressure by saying, "Your sister was reading on a sixth grade level when she was your age" or "Your brother was always good at math." Developmental differences can make some subjects and tasks much more difficult for some children than for others. Comparing a child's academic, musical, athletic, or artistic skills with those of a sibling is neither helpful nor kind.

Parents can continue to answer their children's questions honestly and in the same spirit in which the questions were asked. Parents can respect their child's need for privacy. They can give their child a pet and discuss the process of reproduction using the pet as an example. Grade school children are usually able to make the connection between what they see in their pets and what happens in human life.

When young grade school children come home with off-color jokes or words, parents can use these jokes and words as teachable moments, turning a potentially upsetting episode into a positive one. The child is not helped when parents act shocked and horrified to hear these words. Neither does it help to give the impression that using such language is cute. Instead, parents can ask children if they understand what the word or joke means and explain any misconceptions. They can discuss why sexual jokes and the use of sex-related profanity can be painful to people. They can help their children find ways other than using sexually aggressive language to express feelings of frustration and anger.

Nine Through Twelve Years of Age

DIFFERENCES BETWEEN BOYS AND GIRLS

The average twelve-year-old girl is taller, heavier, and two years closer to physical maturity than the average twelve-year-old boy. Girls usually experience a marked growth spurt at age ten or eleven, while boys grow more quickly around age twelve or thirteen. Boys continue to demonstrate more strength and physical ability.

One seemingly common characteristic at this age is that in mixed-sex situations, girls usually seem unwilling to compete with boys. For example, studies of children from very different cultural groups found that girls were much less competitive when playing dodge ball against boys than they were when playing against other girls, even when both had equal experience. Some girls, when playing with other girls, were measured to have high playing skills. But when playing with boys these girls were likely to stand with their legs crossed and their arms folded, or to talk to one another instead of paying attention to the game. As a result, when playing in mixed-sex games, the boys almost invariably won, even when low-skilled boys played against high-skilled girls.

Boys and girls during this period tend to have larger circles of friends than they did when they were younger. Some are beginning to admire members of the opposite sex, with girls more interested in boys than boys are in girls, but most choose to play and talk with members of their own sex. Girls' relationships often appear to have more complexities, with emotional quarrels, jealousy over sharing friends, and criticism of one another.

By the upper elementary grades boys may appear to have superior mathematical ability and to do better in visual-spatial activities such as manipulating objects in a three-dimensional space or reading maps. Girls often appear to excel at reading comprehension, vocabulary, and verbal creativity. Research in these areas continues. Some recent studies support the conclusion that these differences are based on ability, while others suggest the cause is cultural expectation and bias.

People have recently begun to discard some traditional but unjustified ideas concerning the differences between boys and girls. Eleanor Maccoby and Carolyn Jacklin[6], after careful review of numerous experimental studies with boys and girls, have concluded that several generalizations are without support. Here are some examples:

- Boys have a greater motivation to achieve.
- Girls have a lower self-esteem than boys.
- Boys are better at complex tasks.
- Girls are better at simple, repetitive tasks.
- Boys are less social than girls.
- Boys are more responsive to visual stimuli, and girls are more responsive to what they hear.

STAGES IN SEXUAL DEVELOPMENT

Nine- through twelve-year-olds have an increased interest in sex, although they ask fewer questions than younger children do. Their interests are kept more private. Masturbation and sex play may occur, but not openly, and young persons who masturbate frequently may feel worried or guilty about it. Children this age may experience a lot of peer pressure to be able to tell and understand the humor of off-color jokes. They may also be interested in viewing R-rated movies and television shows.

During this pre-adolescent stage young persons are more likely to talk to friends about sex than to parents. Studies show that while mothers and daughters do talk some, few conversations about sex occur between mothers and sons, fathers and sons, or fathers and daughters. If parents have not been open to their children's sex-related questions, the children are going to find it difficult to talk about their feelings and may be easily embarrassed.

Since homosexual issues are often discussed in the media, and particularly since AIDS has become an important health issue, children may be curious about homosexuality. They may have misunderstandings and worries, especially if they have had strong feelings toward adults or peers of the same sex, or if they have engaged in sex play with same-sex friends. Parents can assure their sons and daughters that curiosity about or attraction to people of the same sex is not in itself an indication of homosexuality.

Even as early as eight, nine, or ten, some children may be coming into physical maturity. Some girls will begin to menstruate, and some boys will find that their testicles and penis are becoming larger. Some are beginning to experience body changes such as the growth of pubic hair, the development of breasts, or the deepening of the voice. Boys may begin to have more frequent erections and may experience nocturnal emissions. Some children will resent the physical changes taking place; some will feel self-conscious and embarrassed. Most will look forward to taking on an adult appearance and may be concerned if they lag behind friends in reaching physical maturity.

Studies by Sandra Weiss[9] have found that older grade school children still need to be hugged and held by their parents. When parents—and especially fathers—touch their children in an intentional, loving manner, the result tends to be children who have good feelings about their bodies.

Other studies have found that as children become older, their need to be in close human contact appears to increase. Despite their attempts to reject affection, adolescents need to be touched or cuddled. Being held helps them relax, reduces anxiety, and provides a sense of security. Unfortunately, the older children become, the less likely parents are to hold and touch them. Often parents shy away from contact with their maturing children, afraid that hugs may be inappropriate or that they might even be rejected. A possible reason for early sexual activity may be the increasing need that boys and girls have for physical contact and the decreasing availability of such contact in the family.

Older grade school students may be interested in the scientific facts related to sex. They may ask general rather than personal questions and may appreciate reading books or leaflets on the subject. They may also be curious about pornography as an alternate source of information, especially if sex is not a subject of open discussion at home.

THE INTERNET CHALLENGE

With the advent of the Internet, pornography has not only become more accessible, it has become almost inescapable. Internet porn, as with other forms of pornography, can present a distorted, unhealthy view of sex and sexuality. Sex devoid of compassion; sex in which persons are demeaned and used; and sex designed to shock viewers' senses rather than to express love—all present particular challenges for parents. Children who view pornography are simply expressing curiosity. Parents may be tempted to react with shock or anger, but what's more important is for parents to model healthy relationships and communicate openly with their children about pornography. If parents have learned that their children are surfing inappropriate sites on the web, they need not overreact, but can quietly use the discovery of such material as an opportunity to open a discussion.

Remember that the chief difference between healthy sexuality and sexuality reflected in pornography is in its intent. A beautiful work of art by

Titian or Ingres, for example, may portray nudity with the intent to communicate the beauty of the human body, or point to a deeper spiritual value through the use of the human form. Pornography, on the other hand, may also portray nudity, but its intent is far different. It communicates disrespect, selfish lust, the callous use of another human being, and even anger. Helping children understand the difference between the two can go a long way toward teaching children positive attitudes toward the human body, healthy passion, and sex.

Finally, Internet pornography can be controlled. Several companies offer downloadable software designed to block most pornography from young surfers. Here are just a few of the more popular sites for downloading such software:

http://www.netnanny.com
http://www.solidoak.com/cysitter.htm
http://www1.surfwatch.com
http://www.cyberpatrol.com

Your web browser (Netscape, Internet Explorer) also contains settings that can limit incoming material. Check your browser's manual or help menu for more information.

Some cities offer Internet Service Providers (ISPs) that block questionable sites at the server site so that subscribers don't have to worry about pornography getting through to your computer.

The best defense against pornography, however, is education. Talking freely and openly with your children about what you value in human relationships, and modeling those values in your everyday lives, will help children understand why pornography is harmful. Your living example will also offer children a positive, healthy alternative to the barrage of images they will inevitably encounter as they grow.

PROVIDING A SOLID BASIS FOR CHILDREN'S SEXUALITY

Parents of pre-adolescents see their children growing taller and starting to develop mature bodies, and the parents may worry that their sons or daughters will grow up too soon. They hear stories of ten-year-old girls giving birth and wonder how much their own children understand about sexual intercourse. There are so many things they want their children to know, yet it seems to be getting more difficult to talk. What can a parent do?

Parents can resist the temptation to tease their sons or daughters about physical changes. Children are very sensitive about their bodies. They are often perplexed and feel self-conscious and unsure of themselves. This doesn't mean that humor has no place. Humor can make conversations about sexuality and body changes go much easier. Parents may want to share humorous experiences they had growing up. As with any subject, humor is fine, as long as it isn't at somebody else's expense.

One of the developmental tasks of adolescence is to rebel against authority. So it makes sense for parents to be sure that pre-teens receive the information they will need to make wise choices as teens.
In addition to giving them needed information, parents of nine- through twelve-year-olds can help their children learn how to say no. Children of all ages need to understand that their bodies are their own and that they don't have to let others touch them. That strong sense of self equips them to resist the peer pressure to engage in sexual intercourse before they are ready. Allow them to practice making good decisions by giving them the freedom to make choices in other areas.

Since children and youth need physical contact, remember to embrace our sons and daughters more frequently. In our family no excuse is needed for hugging our children at any time. We have also found that a back rub or foot massage is almost always appreciated by every member of our family.

We can encourage positive self-images in our children. We can help girls feel good about being women by encouraging them to stand up for themselves. Our daughters need to know that putting themselves down, particularly in comparison to boys, doesn't enhance femininity. It is not unfeminine to be successful, or to be a good athlete, or to be competitive. But it can injure one's self-esteem to say, "I feel like I shouldn't win, so I won't even try." If girls do this frequently in sports, a similar negative attitude may carry over into other male-female relationships. We can encourage our sons to welcome competition from girls, rather than to feel threatened by it. We can also discourage excessive competitiveness between male peers. Boys may need extra convincing of their worth simply because they are who they are and not because they are better than another boy.

As our children get older, it becomes less and less appropriate to say, "This is the way everyone your age acts," "This is what everyone your age thinks," or "This is how everyone your age feels." By sixth grade, girls and boys represent a wide range of developmental levels and personal interests, making it impossible to describe the typical twelve-year-old. Moms and dads observe their children and, knowing that each is unique, encourage the development of their personal identities. Yet it is not unusual for boys and girls to worry about being different. All persons need assurance that they are normal and will be accepted by their friends and by their society.

The openness and support of their parents can make it easier for children to be themselves. Often when a parent plays favorites or demands that their children conform to their standard for proper behavior, the parents are more concerned about how the children will appear to others than with the child's sense of identity. An example of this is the story of Jacob and Esau, found in Genesis 25 and 27. Although Jacob and Esau were twins, their appearance, interests, and personalities were worlds apart. Esau had a red complexion, thick hair, a hearty appreciation of the open country, and the tendency to act impulsively. To Isaac, the boys' father, Esau was a man after his own heart. Jacob had a lighter, smooth complexion, preferred the quietness of staying near home, and tended to analyze a situation before taking action. Jacob was the favorite of his mother, Rebekah.

Rebekah was worried that Jacob would not receive the blessing and acknowledgment she felt that he deserved from his father. She insisted that Jacob pretend to have the physical characteristics and even the typical smell of a real man of the earth, thus tricking Isaac into believing that he was Esau. When Esau came home and discovered that he had been cheated, he asked the heart-rending question that all parents need to take seriously:

> *"Have you only one blessing, father? Bless me, me also, father!" (Genesis 27:38).*

We need to support our children in their uniqueness and not force them into the mold of the average girl or boy. We should affirm their search to identify what masculinity and femininity mean to them personally, instead of fathers saying, "If you want to be a man, you must be just like me," or mothers, "If you want to be a woman, you must be just like me."

A PRAYER FOR UNDERSTANDING

O God,

What a responsibility and privilege it is to be a parent. As the psalmist says, children are a gift from God. Help us to be worthy parents!

Enable us to appreciate the differences between boys and girls. Help us to recognize and to seize opportunities to affirm our children as sexual beings. Give us wisdom and understanding at each stage of their development so that we might be enhancers, not destroyers, of their healthy sexual identities.

Amen.

CHAPTER 4

The Question Box
Part 1–Questions About Sex

HOW CAN I MAKE TALKS WITH MY CHILDREN GO MORE EASILY?

Many parents are frightened by the prospect of talking about sex. We are embarrassed and uncomfortable, concerned that our knowledge and expertise are inadequate. How could we possibly say that word? How can we ever explain that in a way that a child could understand? What if our children bring up the subject of sex during a family holiday meal or at another inappropriate time? What if we give them the wrong ideas? What if they decide to misuse the sexual information they are given?

Children can be unpredictable. We must be prepared to both respond to their questions and to initiate conversations when questions aren't asked. There are some practical things we can do to make sexuality discussions with our children go more easily. Children will feel more secure in talking when they sense our warmth and openness. We can demonstrate a positive attitude toward life in general and toward sex in particular. We can listen carefully to our children's questions and take their concerns seriously. That's sound advice for good communication on any subject.

Matthew gives a beautiful picture of Jesus' openness to children. Jesus wanted the children to be with him, liked to hold them, and became irritated with people who considered them a nuisance. "Let the little children come to me, and do not stop them; for it is to such as these that the kingdom of heaven belongs" (Matthew 19:14). "Whoever welcomes one such child in my name welcomes me" (Matthew 18:5). Jesus loved and respected children. We show by our words and actions that we love and respect our children. We can be available for them, call them to us, stand up for them, and surround them with loving, gentle arms and prayers.

Some parents who find it easy to talk about almost anything else may discover that the topic of sex throws them into a panic. Many adults have been taught that sex is a taboo subject. If this sounds like you, it may help to realize that you are not obligated to tell your children about your personal sex life. You can talk about sexuality openly and still be discreet. If you're feeling nervous, it may be a clue about your own feelings regarding sex. Try not to let your uneasiness or nervousness be a reason to avoid talking with your child, especially when he or she asks you a question. Your child looks up to you and needs to know what you think and what you feel. Try to relax and be yourself. How would you respond to any other question? If you feel embarrassed, just recognize that it's a common feeling for most of us, and press on.

When children come to you with questions, make sure you understand what it is they want to know. Listen carefully, and don't over-anticipate. Remember the story in which a small child asks, "Where did I come from?" The mother launches into a full-scale description of the reproductive process, then asks, "But, Johnny, why did you want to know?" Johnny replies, "Well, Henry said he came from Kalamazoo." It is easy to give our children answers to questions they weren't even asking.

All times and settings are not conducive to conversations about sexuality. Children do not always realize that certain words are not normally discussed or used in public. You may be at a church function, with the pastor sitting on one side of your family and an elderly widow sitting on the other, when your youngster decides to ask you the meaning of a particular slang term. When this happens to us, we give a brief explanation, then firmly but kindly say, "I will tell you more about it when we get home. This isn't the best time." If "best times" are provided on a regular basis, children will learn to save their questions for such moments.

We have also found that it helps to give private attention to each child's questions. We do this for several reasons. One is that Kathy and Timmy are four years apart in age. Timothy may not be interested in Kathryn's concerns or may not be able to understand the answers we give her. Girls and boys may feel embarrassed to talk about personal issues with a sibling of the opposite sex present, especially if they can't trust that other person not to giggle or tease (and brothers and sisters are notorious for both). At the same time, the advantage of such discussions is that it responds to the curiosity that boys have about girls, and girls have about boys.

In our society fathers seem to have a harder time discussing sexual issues with their children than mothers do. Surveys by sociologist Susan Bennett[1] indicate that American fathers assume little responsibility for their children's sex education. In general mothers talk some with their daughters, and less with their sons. Father-daughter and father-son conversations are usually negligible. However, Bennett found that where fathers and mothers share the tasks of discipline, childcare, and household chores, there is a significantly more favorable environment for sex education. So Mom can make sexuality talks with the children go more easily by encouraging Dad to help with the diapers, dishes, and discipline; to assist with homework; and to tuck their sons and daughters into bed.

WHAT WORDS DO YOU USE?

Sometimes the hardest thing in talking about sex is choosing the right words. Many parents avoid using the proper terms, simply because they have not had the opportunity to practice actually saying those terms out loud. They may mislabel acts, saying, "They are sleeping together" instead of "They are having sexual intercourse," or "Do you need to wee-wee?" instead of "Do you need to urinate?" Sometimes parents will use no specific word at all, but just say, "Don't do that" or "Don't touch that."

We can teach even our young children to use correct terms for their body parts. Explanation of slang and street language helps children to connect it with the proper terminology. Parents should not use difficult words simply for the purpose of being scientifically accurate. Accurate information may not be accurately understood, especially when a child is young. Be clear, direct, and matter-of-fact. If you use a difficult word, make certain the child knows what you are talking about. Don't give long, involved explanations. Remember that your tone of voice, facial expression, how close you sit together, and whether or not you are touching all convey a message as well.

A good answer to a question about sex is one that uses words children clearly understand. A good answer addresses the feelings that are part of growing up. It will have heart, not simply facts.

WHAT ABOUT GIVING MY CHILD A BOOK?

Adults who feel uncomfortable talking about sex may think: "I'll give my child a book instead!" They may have the book waiting in a drawer, ready to bring out when their child asks the first question. "Here, read this," they will say, thrusting the book into the child's hands and racing for safety in another room.

Giving children books to read on their own could imply, "We don't talk about these things." Books can be a valuable tool, but should not be a substitute for discussions. Parents can use books on sexuality to bring up topics, to answer questions, or to clarify any misunderstandings. A good book should comfort and inform both you and your child about sexuality. If you feel more secure using a book, why not sit down with your child to read and discuss it together? Cuddle close as you read. By your embrace your child will be able to see that this is an inviting topic, not a frightening one.

Many excellent resources, ranging from picture books about new babies to detailed biological textbooks, are available in bookstores and in the public library. When choosing a book about sex for your child, look for one that gives accurate information, is appropriate for the child's age, treats sexuality with dignity, does not perpetuate myths, and does not talk down to the child. The list of recommended resources at the end of this book lists several titles that we recommend.

Where Did I Come From?, by Peter Mayle, Arthur Robins, and Paul Walter, is a popular, delightful book for children that gets right to the point using no-nonsense language and downright hilarious (though factual) illustrations. It's great for reading together and deals forthrightly with everything from erections and orgasms (like a sneeze??) to the birth of a baby. If this book doesn't get you into the subject with a smile on your face, nothing will! Ages 8 and up.

Created by God: About Human Sexuality for Older Girls and Boys is a companion resource to BEFORE THEY ASK (both published by Abingdon Press). It offers basic information about sex and human development, setting this information in the context of Christian values and positive human relationships. Children who love to read may be interested in fictional books that discuss sexuality issues. Judy Blume's *Are You There God? It's Me, Margaret* is the story of a girl's anxieties about puberty. Blume's *Then Again, Maybe I Won't* presents the problems of adolescent boys. *The Man Without a Face*, by Isabelle Holland, deals with homosexuality.

If your child is reading one of these books, read along, raise questions concerning the characters' values, emotions, and behaviors, and be available to discuss your child's questions.

FACT-GIVING— DOES IT WORK?

Parents sometimes wonder if talking to their children about sexuality will do any good. Does giving our kids the facts ensure that they won't experiment with sexual intercourse before they are married? Does sex education guarantee that they will form positive relationships with persons of the opposite sex later in life, or that they will make good choices concerning the use of birth control?

A survey by the Alan Guttmacher Institute shows that teens who had received formal sex education training were no more likely to be sexually active than those who had not. Sex education will not cause a person to go out and experiment with sex. But students who had sex education were more likely to use contraceptives and were less likely to become pregnant. Parents may say, "But I don't want my children to use contraceptives. I don't want them having intercourse until they are married." We too share that desire for our daughter and son. Going to church doesn't mean children won't be interested in sex. Research confirms that students who have a faith and attend church regularly are no less likely to have sexual intercourse than other students.

Fact-giving alone is not enough, but it is important. Our children will learn about sex, if not from parents, then from their friends, music, television, movies, and the web. Much of the information that they learn will be inaccurate and misleading. We must see that they receive correct information upon which to build responsible decision-making.

The greatest risk of out-of-wedlock pregnancy occurs among adolescents who have been having sexual relationships for only a few months. Adolescents often resent adult intrusion and, once sexual activity has begun, communication might be almost impossible. That's why our sons and daughters need to know the facts about sex while they are still in grade school.

There is more to sexuality training than teaching biological facts. Our children need to be aware of the emotions and desires that they will have as they mature, and know how to manage them. We want our children to form positive values, to realize that sexuality is a major area of vulnerability, and to understand that sex should not be used for destructive or exploitative purposes. We want them to feel good about themselves, to be sensitive to the needs and feelings of others, and to be able to love.

HOW MUCH INFORMATION IS TOO MUCH?

Parents can't expect to cover all of the important things they want to say about sex in one setting. Sex education is not a one-session event, but a lifetime process. We have the freedom, then, to decide that "this is enough information for now." If we are discussing a question with our child, and he or she begins to fidget and lose interest, it is probably time to go on to something else. Young children do not have long attention spans and may not be able to concentrate on lengthy explanations.

Remember that there are stages in the development of children's understanding of sex and birth. Five-year-olds don't think in the same way that ten-year-olds do. If we give children information that is geared to a higher level of understanding, they may not be able to put the facts all together. Too many details will be confusing.

If your child becomes embarrassed or upset during a discussion, change to a less-threatening topic and return to your talk at another time. Ask questions to find out what the child is thinking before you attempt to give any more information. Remember, your own comfort level sends a strong message to your children. The more mentionable sex is to you, the more manageable it will be for your children.

We have a list of "Don'ts" that we feel are important for parents to remember when talking with children about sex. Don't use sex to frighten your children, such as the old masturbation myths of blindness or sterility. Don't start by telling fables such as "The stork brought you" or other untruths. Don't tease your child about sexuality. Don't punish your child if he engages in sex play or asks embarrassing questions. And don't be emotionally dishonest yourself—examine your attitudes and feelings and accept the range of emotions that you might feel.

WHAT IF MY CHILD NEVER ASKS QUESTIONS?

Some parents worry about the answers that they should give to their children's questions. Other parents worry because their children never seem to have any questions to be answered. What should parents do if their children never ask questions about sex?

We don't have to wait for our children to bring up the subject. We can use the opportunities of everyday life to talk about sexual issues. These "teachable moments" are the innumerable small situations that might occur at any time—moments that we can use as springboards for sharing our thoughts and values. Talk about Aunt Carolyn's new baby. Stop at the window of the pet shop to admire the new puppies. Look at the lingerie section in the J.C. Penney catalog. Discuss the evening news. Comment on how tall your children are growing or how mature they appear to be. Watch TV with your children and ask them what they think or how they feel about some of the "sexy" scenes. The possibilities are endless. The trick for parents is learning how to recognize and take advantage of these opportunities.

In our family we have found that the perfect time to talk about sex is not programmed. Our most productive discussions occur while driving in the car, while eating an after-school snack, while taking a bath, or when it is time to go to sleep. We have never specifically set aside a time to talk about sex. But we do ask our children questions such as, "How do the boys in your class feel about the girls?" "How do you think mommies get to be mommies?" "Do you want to be a daddy when you grow up?" A child's unexpected entrance when we are using the bathroom or changing clothes can be used to talk about the adult body. We include our children in adult discussions of the news, so that in talking about AIDS, homosexuality, marital infidelity, or child abuse, we can listen to our children's feelings and worries, as well as help them learn about human sexuality.

Sometimes what we don't say communicates our values and attitudes toward sex. Intentionally redirecting conversation away from sex when it may be appropriate to discuss it sends the message that sex is a taboo subject. Overreacting when a child wanders into our room while we're changing clothes can send the message that bodies are shameful. It's worth considering our own attitudes toward sex and sexuality when instances like these arise.

Part II–Questions and Sample Responses

No two children are exactly alike—each has a unique set of interests, questions, and worries. No two parents are alike, either. Parents all have their own styles of responding to children—styles that build on their personal sets of values and experiences. There is no one correct way to talk with a child about sexuality. But it can sometimes be informative to "eavesdrop" on the conversations of other parents and children, if only to discover the variety of questions and possible responses that exist. On the following pages you will find a series of questions that children at different age levels might ask, and a short response that might be offered. These are not intended to be the only or even the best possible responses. But we hope they will encourage you to think ahead about the answers you may someday want to give to your children.

As you read some of the responses, you may find them too complicated. Children will probably not be able to understand all of this information, especially the first time they hear it. Children are often curious about topics that are difficult to explain in simple terms. Do not underestimate your child, however. He or she may be able to grasp much more than you realize.

QUESTIONS PRESCHOOL CHILDREN MIGHT ASK

Young children, fascinated with babies, might wonder:

Where was I kept before you married Daddy?

You weren't kept anywhere because you didn't exist yet. To make a baby, you need a man and woman to be the baby's father and mother. A new baby is created from an ovum inside the mother and a sperm from the father.

How does the baby get inside the mother?

The mother's body makes an ovum. The father's body makes a sperm, which he places into the mother's body with his penis. When the ovum and the sperm cell join together, a baby starts to grow.

Do unmarried people ever have babies?

Yes. Sometimes they do. You don't have to be married to have a baby, but it does take both a man and a woman in order for the baby to be formed.

Can a man be pregnant with a baby?

No. Men's bodies are different from women's bodies. Mothers have a special place, called the uterus, for the baby. Mothers also have a special passage inside their bodies, called the vagina, where the baby comes out when it is ready. Men and boys do not have a uterus or vagina.

Can a baby cry before it is born?

No. An unborn baby doesn't cry. In order to make the sound of crying, you have to have air in your lungs. This air moves up into your voice box to make the crying sound. But a baby doesn't use its lungs for breathing until after it is born, so it can't cry.

Does the baby come out through the belly button?

No. A baby comes out of the mother through her vagina, which is between her legs.

Where does the milk come from when you nurse the baby?

The mother's body makes the milk for her baby. The milk is formed by special glands in her breasts.

Tucking a pillow under her shirt and pretending to be pregnant, a child announces, "I want to have my own baby now. Why can't I?"

Your body isn't ready to have babies. As you grow older, your body will change so that you could have a baby if you chose to.

Daddy, I'm going to marry you when I grow up!

You must think I'm somebody special to want to marry me. Thank you! Lots of boys and girls think about the same thing. But you can't marry me because I am your father. When you grow up, you can fall in love with a man and get married to him. If you have children, he will be their father, and I will be their grandfather!

Preschool children have questions about their bodies and about differences between boys and girls. They may want to know:

Why don't girls have a penis?

Girls' bodies are different from boys' bodies. Girls have a vulva, which is the part of a girl's body that is between her legs.

Why are boys' bathrooms different from girls' bathrooms?

When you urinate, the fluid comes out of the urethra. A girl's urethra is inside her body, so it is easier for her to urinate while sitting. A boy's urethra is in his penis, and he can urinate standing up. This is why boys' and girls' bathrooms are different—boys' bathrooms often have urinals to use while standing, and girls' bathrooms do not.

Daddy has a scratchy beard. Why doesn't Mommy?

When men and boys grow up, hair grows on their faces. Women don't grow lots of hair on their faces, even after they become adults.

What is the belly button for?

People get energy by eating healthy food and breathing oxygen. But unborn babies can't eat or breathe, so the mother must share her food and fresh air with her baby through a tube called an umbilical cord. It connects at the baby's tummy. After babies are born, they begin breathing and eating on their own, so they don't need the umbilical cord anymore. It is tied and cut near the baby's tummy (no, it doesn't hurt at all), and it leaves the indention called the navel or belly button. Your navel doesn't do anything now—it just marks the spot where you were once connected to your mother.

QUESTIONS YOUNGER ELEMENTARY STUDENTS MIGHT ASK

Younger grade school students have many questions about the human body, such as:

Why do grownups have so much hair on their bodies?

When a person's body becomes mature or grownup, it produces chemicals called hormones. Hormones cause hair to grow. Both men and women have hair under their arms, on their legs, and in their genital areas (around the sex organs). Men also have hair on their faces and often on their chests.

Why do women menstruate? What is a period?

Menstruation, commonly called a period, is one part of the reproductive cycle—which means it is part of the way a woman's body gets ready to have a baby. About once a month, an ovum is released by the ovaries. The uterus begins to build up a rich lining of blood and tissue, which will serve as a bed to help the ovum grow. Most of the time the ovum is not fertilized by a sperm cell. Since there is no baby in the uterus, this lining is not needed. Menstruation is when the blood and tissue from the uterus flow out of the body.

What are the testicles for?

The testicles are the male glands that produce the sperm cells. The testicles also produce the male sex hormones that cause body changes such as the growth of the penis, the appearance of pubic hair, and a deeper voice.

What is circumcision?

The skin on the penis of a newborn baby boy covers the end of his penis. This skin is sometimes removed in an operation called circumcision. The operation is usually done shortly after he is born. Some boys are not circumcised. Circumcised and uncircumcised penises look different, but they work just the same.

Grade school students may wonder about terms that are unfamiliar to them, especially if they hear these words used in movies or TV or by their friends:

What is a virgin? Can a boy be a virgin?

A virgin is someone who has not had sexual intercourse. Both boys and girls can be virgins.

What is a prostitute?

A prostitute is someone who is paid for taking part in a sexual act.

What is a homosexual?

Homosexuals are persons who are sexually attracted to or sexually active with other persons of the same sex. Women homosexuals are called lesbians; male homosexuals are often referred to as gay.

Younger elementary students are often curious about the act of sexual intercourse:

Why do people have sex? Why would they want to?

Sexual intercourse is a way that two people can demonstrate their love for one another. It can provide great physical pleasure and closeness and is also the way to have children.

What happens during sexual intercourse?

Before a man and woman have sexual intercourse, the man's penis becomes larger and more firm. This is called an erection. The woman's vagina becomes wet and relaxed. Intercourse takes place when the man pushes his penis into the woman's vagina, and they move their bodies together. The man usually experiences an ejaculation, where a fluid, called semen (which contains sperm) is squirted from his penis. If a sperm cell joins with an ovum in the woman's body, a baby begins. A baby does not begin, however, every time they have intercourse.

What is birth control?

Birth control means choosing whether or when to have a baby.

> **Grade school students are still very interested in babies and in pregnancy:**

How does a cell turn into a baby?

When the ovum joins with a sperm cell, it is fertilized. The fertilized ovum then begins the process of cell division. The cell divides into two cells. Then each of those cells divides into two, and so on. Some of the cells will eventually develop into fingers, toes, and all the rest of the baby's body.

What causes twins?

When one fertilized ovum divides into two completely separate cells, twins will develop. These twins will look almost exactly alike, so they are called identical twins. There is also another way that twins are formed. Sometimes two separate ova (more than one ovum) join with two different sperm, and then each of them begins to develop into a new human being. These twins will not look exactly the same, but differ just like regular brothers and sisters differ from each other. We call them fraternal twins.

Why does a baby look like its parents?

The ovum, which comes from the baby's mother, and the sperm, which comes from the father, both contain chromosomes with genes. The genes carry "messages" to the newly formed child. The combination of genes that you receive from your parents determines what you will look like. You will be like one parent in some ways and like the other parent in other ways. You will also have features that are blends of both.

What decides a baby's sex?

The sex chromosomes do. The sex chromosome that carries instructions for being male is called a Y chromosome, and the sex chromosome that carries instructions for being female is called an X chromosome. If a baby has two X chromosomes, it is a girl. But if a baby has a combination of an X and a Y chromosome, it is a boy.

How can you tell if a baby is going to be a girl or a boy?

Years ago, parents often did not know whether their child was a boy or girl until the moment the baby was born. However, doctors today can use sound vibrations (called ultrasound) to look at the baby on a monitor before it is born, and the ultrasound pictures often show the doctor and the parents what the baby's sex is.

How long does it take for a baby to be formed?

It takes about 280 days (nine months) for a baby to develop.

How does a woman know she is going to have a baby?

A woman can often guess that she is going to have a baby when she misses a menstrual period, and if she feel nauseous (called having morning sickness). The doctor can test the woman's urine to see if it shows traces of hormones from the baby.

Can a baby hear before it is born?

Yes. The unborn baby can probably hear voices, the beat of the mother's heart, and the noise of music and traffic outside.

How does a baby breathe inside the mother?

The umbilical cord carries oxygen to the baby from the placenta.

How does a baby "go to the bathroom" before he is born?

The umbilical cord carries wastes away from the baby.

How is a baby actually born?

The woman's vagina expands, and as muscles contract or suddenly get shorter, they begin to push the baby out. These contractions are called labor. The baby comes down through the mother's cervix (the opening of the uterus), usually head-first.

How long does labor usually take?

It depends. First babies usually take longer to be born. Labor may take as long as 10 to 16 hours or more.

Does labor hurt?

Yes. Labor contractions are painful for mothers. Some parents take childbirth classes to help them learn to control the pain through breathing. Others may use medication to control the pain.

Does the baby ever get stuck?

The labor contractions cause the cervix to open wide enough to allow the baby to pass through. If there is a danger that the baby will have difficulty passing through the birth canal, the doctor may perform an operation called a caesarean section to deliver the baby through the abdomen.

Does cutting the umbilical cord hurt the baby?

No. The umbilical cord has no nerve endings in it, so cutting the cord does not hurt.

What is a miscarriage?

A miscarriage is when a baby is born before it has developed enough to live outside the mother's body. It usually occurs when something has happened to interfere with the fetus's normal growth.

QUESTIONS OLDER GRADE SCHOOL STUDENTS MIGHT ASK

> Boys and girls have questions about the changes their bodies are (or will soon be) experiencing:

What is the male reproductive system like?

Sperm cells are produced in the testicles, which are held in the scrotum. The scrotum helps to keep the sperm cells at the correct temperature. When it is cold, a small muscle in the scrotum pulls the testicles up close to the body for warmth.

The sperm cells mature as they move through the epididymis—a tiny tube attached to the back of each testicle. Each epididymis connects to its own vas deferens, a tube where the sperm cells are mixed with fluids called semen. The sperm and semen move into the male urethra, a tube in the center of the penis.

When semen is to leave the body, the penis tissue fills with blood, causing the penis to become larger, firmer, and to stand out from the body. This is called an erection. Semen can then be forcefully ejected from the body by contractions of the prostate gland and the seminal vesicles. This is called an ejaculation.

Does an ejaculation happen with every erection?

No. The penis can become erect for reasons besides sexual stimulation, such as when lifting a heavy load, wearing clothing that is tight, having to urinate, or even for no apparent reason at all. These erections usually go away after a few minutes.

Why do boys have "wet dreams"?

As a boy's body begins to physically mature, it constantly produces sperm. The sperm accumulates in the tubes leading from the testes. When excess sperm has accumulated, the body gets rid of it by an ejaculation of semen, often during sleep. This ejaculation is called a nocturnal emission or wet dream. It may or may not be accompanied by sex-related dreams.

Is semen the same as urine?

No. Urine is a yellowish liquid body waste that is formed in the kidneys and stored in the bladder. Semen is a thick, whitish fluid that carries sperm cells from the testicles. Both urine and semen leaves the body through the urethra, but never at the same time.

Is it normal for one testicle to be bigger or to hang lower in the scrotum than the other?

Yes. One testicle—usually the left one—normally hangs lower than the other. This is a way that the body has to protect the testicles from being painfully pressed together. If one or both of the testicles has not descended into the scrotum, a doctor should correct the situation.

Does the size of the penis make a difference?

Boys and men often worry about how tall they are, how muscular they are, how much hair they have on their bodies, and about the size of their genitals. They compare themselves to other boys and men and, if they are smaller or have less hair, may begin feeling bad about themselves. The size of the penis is not related to sexual capability, but it can be related to how one feels about his body. It's something you don't have any control over, so it is best to accept your body as it is. These feelings are very common. No one your age wants to feel different. You're not alone.

What is the female reproductive system like?

A woman has two ovaries, each about the size of a pecan, in the lower part of her abdomen. The ovaries hold the ovum or ova. About once a month one of the ovaries will release an ovum—this is called ovulation. The ovum enters one of the fallopian tubes, where it may be fertilized by a sperm cell from a male. The fallopian tubes lead to the uterus, a hollow organ about three inches long. If an ovum is fertilized, it implants itself onto the wall of the uterus and grows there, with the uterus stretching to make room for the fetus. The lower part of the uterus is the cervix. When babies are born, they are generally delivered through the vagina.

When will I begin to menstruate?

A girl usually begins to menstruate sometime between the ages of 10 and 14. Some girls begin before this, and others may be 16 or 17 before they first menstruate. Menstruation is a sign that you are capable of reproduction.

How do you know when you are about to have your period?

Many girls find that they feel "puffy" or bloated a few days before their periods begin because their bodies retain an extra amount of water. This water can even cause a several-pound weight gain. Some girls may feel irritable, tense, or depressed during this time. Others experience back-aches or slight pain in the uterine area or may find that their breasts are very sensitive to touch.

What is this white stuff that gets on my panties?

A woman's body secretes a white fluid called a vaginal discharge, especially right before the menstrual period or around the time of ovulation. This fluid is caused by bacteria in the vagina that provide natural protection against germs and infections. This is normal. However, if the discharge has an unpleasant odor or causes burning or itching, it is usually caused by an infection and should be treated by a doctor.

Sometimes I "touch myself." Does this mean I am strange or doing something wrong?

No. Obtaining physical pleasure by touching or rubbing our sex organs is called masturbation. It is normal and not harmful unless we become overly preoccupied with it. This is one of the ways that we discover more about our bodies.

Older grade school students have questions about pregnancy and sexual intercourse:

How many times does it take to "do it" before you get pregnant? Can a girl become pregnant the first time?

It only takes one act of sexual intercourse to become pregnant. One does not become pregnant every time she has intercourse.

Is there a certain time when a woman can get pregnant?

A woman is most likely to become pregnant at the time of ovulation (when the ovum is released), and on the days immediately before and after. This occurs approximately 14 days after the beginning of the menstrual cycle.

If you miss your period, does that mean that you are pregnant?

It might, if you have had sexual intercourse. However, stress, illness, losing a large amount of weight, or strenuous exercise can cause a period to be late or missed.

Can you have a baby when you are 10 years old?

The beginning of menstruation is a sign that your body is physically capable of pregnancy. Some 10-year-olds have already reached puberty, and it would be possible for them to have a baby.

Can a girl become pregnant without intercourse?

Usually not. While it is unlikely, pregnancy is possible if semen is ejaculated near the vaginal opening. The semen may seep in without penetration of the penis inside the woman's body. In addition, if a man has semen on his hands when he touches a woman's vagina, the sperm may enter her body in this way.

What kinds of birth control methods are there?

There are many different methods of birth control. The only 100 percent effective method is not to have sexual intercourse. This is called abstinence. Some women take birth control pills, which contain artificial hormones that stop the release of ova.

Other women use an intrauterine device (IUD) made of metal or plastic that a doctor inserts into the uterus. Some women block sperm from entering the uterus by using a diaphragm—a rubber cap that fits over the cervix, or by placing sperm-killing creams or foams into the vagina. A man can wear a condom on his penis during sexual intercourse. A condom is like a large, rolled-up balloon that is unrolled over the penis to catch the sperm. Some couples use Natural Family Planning, which requires couples to watch for signs of ovulation and then to refrain from sexual intercourse on those days when conception is possible. Because of the difficulty of determining exactly when ovulation occurs, this method can be unreliable.

Surgical methods of birth control are called sterilization. A man might have a vasectomy, in which the vas deferens in each testicle is cut and tied; a woman might have a tubal ligation in which her fallopian tubes are cut and tied.

What happens in an abortion?

Abortion is the act of stopping a pregnancy. One method is dilation and curettage (D & C), in which the lining of the uterus is scraped to disconnect the embryo from the uterine wall. Another method is vacuum aspiration, which uses suction to pull the lining and the embryo from the uterine wall.

Does it hurt to have sex with a boy?

Sexual intercourse is generally pleasurable for women and men. As a couple leads up to sexual intercourse, their bodies prepare. Men are ready for intercourse before their partners are ready, and must be patient. If a woman is rushed, intercourse can be painful. The first few experiences of intercourse can be uncomfortable for both the woman and the man—generally due to their nervousness and their inability to relax.

What is rape?

Rape means being forced to have sexual intercourse against your will. It is against the law. Rape by someone with whom you are on a date is referred to as date rape and is also against the law.

What is incest?

Incest is having sexual relations with a blood relative. It is illegal in the United States and forbidden in most parts of the world.

What is STD?

STD stands for Sexually Transmitted Disease—a disease passed through sexual contact. If not treated these diseases can cause mental illness, damage to the heart and other parts of the body, or even death. Common STDs include gonorrhea, syphilis, herpes, trichomoniasis, and chlamydia.

What is AIDS?

AIDS is an abbreviation for Acquired Immune Deficiency Syndrome, a disease that causes a breakdown of the body's system for fighting off disease. AIDS is transmitted through the exchange of body fluids. This takes place during heterosexual or homosexual intercourse with an infected person; through the sharing of contaminated needles by drug users; and from an infected mother to her unborn baby. Some AIDS victims were infected before

76

1985 when they received contaminated blood during a transfusion. Because of improved blood testing procedures, this is extremely unlikely today.

How can a person keep from getting AIDS?

The best way to avoid contracting AIDS is not to have sexual intercourse. Persons who do engage in sexual intercourse should use condoms for protection. Because AIDS is also spread by contaminated needles, you should not use drugs and should never share hypodermic needles.

Can both men and women carry sexually transmitted diseases?

Yes. Both sexes can contract and carry these diseases. A pregnant woman can also pass the disease to her unborn baby.

> **Boys and girls in the upper grade school levels may be beginning to have questions and worries about relationships and emotions:**

What makes me feel so moody?

As you grow, your view of the world changes. You become more aware of what is going on around you. Your family once seemed secure and satisfying and demanded very little from you. But now that you are older, you have greater responsibilities, more concerns about the future, and increased personal insecurity. These can all make you feel moody. In addition your hormones are causing your body to develop, and these hormonal changes can often cause mood swings.

What should I do when someone teases me about my body?

It hurts when someone teases you about being too big or too small or makes fun of the changes your body is going through. Remember that change is normal and good and that everyone develops at his or her own rate. The persons doing the teasing are probably unsure of or frightened by some of their own body changes. If an adult teases you, it may because he or she is not emotionally ready to see you grow up. Try to be understanding, have a good sense of humor, and don't let the teasing damage your positive self-image.

Sometimes I daydream about sexy things. Is there something wrong with me? Does this mean I'm perverted?

Most people have sexual fantasies. Sometimes people have sexual urges and desires, but they know that acting on those urges would be inappropriate, so they just imagine them instead. This can be healthy and helpful. But sometimes people get caught up in their fantasies and are unable to think about anything else. Or they may lose sight of the difference between what is real and what is imaginary and may try to live out their fantasies, hurting themselves and others in the process.

Do many people have sex before marriage? What happens if they do?

While many persons do have sex before marriage, the numbers do not make it advisable or right. There are risks, including emotional hurt, pregnancy, disease, and often it destroys the relationship they thought they would fulfill with intercourse.

How can people control their desire for sex?

People can learn to control their sexual emotions in the same way that they control their other emotions. Toddlers have to learn to control their temper tantrums. Kindergarten children must conquer their fear of going to school. We must discover how to set limits and standards for ourselves, then we must learn to live within those limits. Another way to control our desire for sex is not to allow ourselves to think mainly or exclusively about sex. We can exercise, keep busy, and have other interests, goals, and activities in addition to our interest in sex.

How can I say no?

The best time to decide to say no is before you are under pressure to decide. If someone wants you to have a sexual relationship that you are not ready for or just do not want to have, you have the right to simply say, "No, I don't want to." You do not have to explain or apologize. Remember that the consequences of sexual activity can be long-lasting and life-changing. Be sure that you are ready for those possibilities before you say yes.

Is it ever okay to have sex?

When two people care deeply for each other and have made a commitment to each other, sexual intercourse can be a beautiful expression of their love. It is a way in which a husband and wife can give one another the gift of pleasure and intimacy. It is also the way in which a couple can take part in the creation of a new life.

I think having a baby would be fun! What could be so bad about having a baby when you're my age?

Having a baby is an adult thing to do. It's understandable for young people to want to do adult things. But, while babies are cute and precious, they are also tremendous responsibilities—not toys. They need constant care. It takes thousands of dollars to pay for the food, diapers, and health care they need. When someone as young as you has a child, it is almost always impossible for the mother to earn enough money to provide for the baby's needs. If you had a baby, you would have to grow up very fast and would probably feel cheated out of your own childhood. Also, when the mother is very young, her baby's health can be put in danger—the baby has a much greater chance of being born too early or of having a low birthweight.

Why do our bodies begin to change and mature so long before we are ready to get married and raise a family?

Years ago, people got married at a much younger age. It didn't take years of educational training to prepare them for their life's work, so they often had the means of providing for a family when they were still very young. It was usually helpful for a family to have a large number of children, so a couple would start early to build that family. But today, while better nutrition and health care cause our bodies to mature even earlier than they used to, it takes longer and longer to prepare to live and to work in society as an adult. As a result, the waiting period between the time our bodies are ready for sexual intercourse and the time we are mature enough in other ways seems so long.

Older elementary students have worries about homosexuality and unusual sexual activities or preferences:

If you have a crush on someone of your own sex, does that make you a homosexual?

No. A homosexual is someone who remains sexually attracted only to a person or persons of his or her own sex. One crush or one experience does not make a person a homosexual.

What does AC/DC mean?

AC/DC is a slang term for bisexuality. A bisexual is a person who is sexually attracted to or sexually active with both women and men. The term AC/DC comes from the two different types of electrical current—alternating and direct.

What is a transsexual?

Transsexuals are persons who believe themselves to be one sex mentally and emotionally, while they are the opposite sex physically. Some of these persons undergo sex-change operations to make them more like the sex that they feel they are.

What is oral sex?

Oral sex is when a person uses his or her mouth to stimulate the other partner's genitals.

What is artificial insemination?

Artificial insemination means placing sperm into a woman's vagina by means of a syringe. Doctors may perform artificial insemination when a couple has not been able to conceive a child through sexual intercourse.

What is a surrogate mother?

When a couple wishes to have a baby, but the woman is unable to conceive, they may arrange to have another woman become impregnated with the husband's sperm by artificial insemination. This substitute mother will carry the fetus in her body until its birth. After the child is delivered, he or she is raised by the biological father and his wife.

A TIME FOR SILENCE

No matter how helpful we want to be, we should try not to bombard our sons and daughters with talk. The advice we give to our children is vitally important, but so are the moments of listening. Are we hearing what our children are saying beneath their questions? Do we understand their worries and fears? Can we tell when they are confused or embarrassed? Are we willing to admit when we don't know an answer? Do we assure our kids that we sometimes have questions and worries and that we understand what it means to feel embarrassed and confused? As Ecclesiastes 11:5 says, we are not experts on life.

Just as you do not know how the breath comes to the bones in the mother's womb, so you do not know the work of God, who makes everything.

When our kids ask questions about what it means to be "all grown up," we should be humble! An appropriate response might be, "I don't know. I'm still growing—not my body, but my mind and my relationships." We don't need to feel that we must have an answer for every issue. Sometimes it is all right to be silent. And when we do talk, we should always try to be loving and wise.

In answering our children's questions about sex, the old adage is true— it's not just what you say that matters, but how you say it. We can be evasive or direct, cynical or supportive, critical or nurturing. As Paul says in Ephesians 4:29:

> *Let no evil talk come out of your mouths, but only what is use-*
> *ful for building up, as there is need, so that your words may*
> *give grace to those who hear.*

If this is how we, as parents, choose our words, we can then dare to show our children Proverbs 4. This proverb, which insists that children should listen to what their parents say, is based on the assumption that parents have wisdom. It claims that parental insight brings protection, safety, and love; that knowing the right way to live gives positive direction for decision-making; that education is important to life itself; and that understanding can influence what happens in our life, even affecting our thoughts and our health.

> *Listen, children, to a father's instruction,*
> *and be attentive, that you may gain insight;*
> *for I give you good precepts:*
> *do not forsake my teaching. . . .*
> *Get wisdom; get insight: do not forget, nor turn away*
> *from the words of my mouth.*
> *Do not forsake her, and she will keep you;*
> *love her, and she will guard you.*
> *The beginning of wisdom is this: Get wisdom,*
> *and whatever else you get, get insight. . . .*
> *Hear, my child, and accept my words,*
> *that the years of your life may be many.*
> *I have taught you the way of wisdom;*
> *I have led you in the paths of uprightness.*
> *When you walk, your step will not be hampered;*
> *and if you run, you will not stumble.*
> *Keep hold of instruction; do not let go;*
> *guard her, for she is your life.*
> *My child, be attentive to my words;*
> *inclining your ear to my sayings.*
> *Do not let them escape from your sight;*

keep them within your heart.
For they are life to those who find them,
    and healing to all their flesh.
Keep your heart with all vigilance,
    for from it flow the springs of life. . . .
Let your eyes look directly forward,
    and your gaze be straight before you.
Keep straight the path of your feet,
    and all your ways will be sure.
Do not swerve to the right or to the left;
    turn your foot away from evil.
(Proverbs 4:1-2, 5-7, 10-13, 20-23, 25-27)

These verses can be marvelous guidelines for parents who are answering questions about sex! Do our answers give children the security and love they need to feel protected and affirmed? Will our answers help our sons and daughters make their own decisions? Are we showing our children that they don't need to be afraid of knowledge about sex, because information and understanding can make us stronger, happier, and healthier? If we can honestly answer "yes" to these guidelines, we can "look straight ahead with honest confidence" as we communicate with our children about the important things in life.

A PRAYER FOR WISDOM

Loving God,

Be near me as I talk with my children about our sexuality. Help me relate to them with trust, love, and respect. Show me how to be warm and open in my attitudes as well as my answers.

Help me listen to my child. Grant me the courage to admit my lack of knowledge when confronted with something I don't know, and help me not to be afraid of my own discomfort or embarrassment. Keep me alert to recognize teachable moments, and give me wisdom as I choose my words.

Amen.

CHAPTER 5

The Real World

BOYS AND GIRLS IN A BOX

When we parents take an honest look at the world in which we and our children live, we realize that sexual security is not part of the environment. In many ways, sexuality spells danger for our sons and daughters—danger found in the violence of sexual abuse and rape, the threat of AIDS and other sexually transmitted diseases, the pressure from the media to conform with its images of masculinity and femininity, the use of off-color jokes and sex-related slang terms, the lure of early sexual activity, the possibility of unwanted pregnancies, and general family stress.

As parents, we may want to gather up our children, place them in a protective box, and sit on the lid until we are sure it is safe for them to emerge into the world! We can't do that, of course. Though we want to protect our children from potential dangers, we do not have the option of isolating them. They have to live in a real world complete with real dangers.

How can we, living in a society where people are hurt every day by sex, help our children to face life with a positive attitude? How can we show them that sexuality is a good gift, not a harmful one? The best protection is to be informed. Naivete, ignorance, and fear can trip us and plunge us headlong into sexual pitfalls. Aware of the dangers that exist, we can intentionally work against them.

SEXUAL ABUSE OF CHILDREN

Some of the most startling and troubling statistics of American society show the frequency with which children are being sexually abused. The American Humane Association reports that there were at least 115,000 confirmed cases of child abuse in 1994. Many other cases are suspected, but have not been verified. Research suggests that one-fifth of all girls and one-sixth of all boys will be the victims of sexual abuse before they are 18 years old. Of the confirmed cases involving girls, 30 to 50 percent of the offenders were related to their victim. Only one in ten of the abusers were related to male victims. Many of the other offenders were persons the child knew—a family friend, baby-sitter, or neighbor. Most of the sexually abused children were between seven and twelve years of age. Males make up between 25 and 35 percent of child sexual abuse victims.

Most cases of child molesting and incest occur at night in the home of the offender or victim—not in cars, abandoned buildings, parks, or on the school grounds. Nine out of ten offenders are men, typically under age 31.[1]

Because assailants usually warn their victims not to tell, children who are sexually assaulted are often afraid to report the incident. They worry that they will be punished, blamed, or not believed. Indeed, many parents do blame or punish the child who has been molested. Though they remain silent, sexually abused children may tell in other ways. They may become depressed and withdrawn or may pinch or bite themselves to inflict self-pain. They may mimic the actions of sexual intercourse during their play. Abused children may also appear to be in a daze or want to sleep for extended periods of time. They may regress in behavior, reverting to bed-wetting, thumb sucking, or fearing the dark. School-aged children may do poorly in school, have frequent nightmares, or begin to act out sexually with their toys or pets. Teens who have been sexually abused may become highly emotional and experience intense fears of sexual activity. Others go to the opposite extreme and become deliberately provocative, behaving in ways that make them vulnerable to further sexual attacks. Some run away from home, become suicidal, or turn to drug and alcohol abuse.

The sexual abuse of children is not limited to any type of family or geographical location—it occurs in all racial and ethnic groups and across all economic and social levels. However, certain similarities are frequently evident. Sexually abused children and their families often appear to be socially isolated and have difficulty forming relationships outside the home. Parents in such families are often very strict, set rigid rules for relationships, and appear highly religious. Many have lived in a given community less than two years. Children in such families may be expected to assume unreasonable levels of responsibility.[2]

84

Children suffering from parental abuse may defend the abusive parent. They may worry that exposing the abuse would destroy family unity and happiness. When such children do seek help, they often find themselves isolated, especially if other family members (including the non-abusive parent) continue to support the offender by refusing to believe that the assault occurred.

Sexual abusers frequently deny or rationalize their actions. They may state that fondling a child's genitals is simply a way of expressing parental affection or a means for teaching the child about sex. Many parents who sexually abuse their children were themselves abused as children and may experience difficulty in coming to grips with those past experiences.

HELPING PROTECT YOUR CHILD AGAINST SEXUAL ABUSE

Some parents worry that a discussion of sexual abuse will frighten their child. They decide to keep quiet about the topic, hoping they will never need to face the issue. A study conducted in Boston found that parents from every social sector and ethnic group were uncomfortable dealing with the possibility of sexual abuse and were doing little to educate their children about it.

Helping our children to be sexually safe is just as important as teaching them the basics of fire or traffic safety. Although very young boys and girls are the most easily victimized, they can be taught to protect themselves against sexual abuse. We can teach them that their bodies are good, that their bodies belong to them, and that no one has a right to touch any part of their bodies that they do not want touched. We can tell them that learning to take care of and protect our bodies is a natural part of growing up and that almost every adult wants to help them be safe. Stress to your children the importance of telling someone right away if they have been abused, even if the offender threatens them into secrecy.

There are several books on the market designed to teach children about preventing sexual abuse. One excellent resource is *Red Flag, Green Flag People*, by J. Williams. This story and coloring book teaches children to be alert to possible dangers and to know what "red flags" to watch out for. Other resources, such as puppet plays and skits, have been developed for use in schools and day care centers. Most are designed to educate the boys and girls in a lighthearted, entertaining, and non-threatening manner, and have been used with excellent results. Encourage your school or church to investigate the use of such programs for their students.

HELPING A CHILD WHO HAS BEEN SEXUALLY ABUSED

What should you do if your child tells you that he or she has been sexually abused? First, believe the child and take the complaint seriously. Children do not usually lie about being molested. Second, assure the child that the episode is all right to talk about and was not something for which he or she is to blame. Children in such situations need to know that they are believed and that you will do everything possible to make sure the abuse stops. Focus on the emotions and needs of the child, not on the anger you feel towards the assailant. Do your best to make the child feel secure and to help him or her maintain a positive self-image.

A sexually abused child needs to receive immediate medical attention, given the possibility of physical damage and the great risk of contracting a sexually transmitted disease. Realize that the medical exam itself may be traumatic for the child and try to see that he or she feels safe and understands what is happening. If possible, use a doctor your child already knows and with whom he or she feels comfortable.

The law requires that you report suspected cases of child abuse. Contact the Human Services or Sexual Abuse Unit of your local police department, County Social Services, or call the National Abuse Hotline: 1-800-422-4453 (1-800-4A CHILD).

RAPE AND INCEST: THE BIBLE TOUCHES A SAD TRUTH

Sexual violence is not just a modern phenomenon. Numerous Bible stories attest to the sad truth that rape and incest have been with us for thousands of years. Bible stories often depict a lust that escalates into an act of hostile violence. In 2 Samuel 13 and 14, David's son Amnon was tormented with desire for his beautiful sister, Tamar. Urged on by his friend Jonadab, Amnon planned the rape of his sister—an act viewed as an offense against the entire family. David was angry, as was Tamar's other brother, Absalom. After two years of letting his hatred for Amnon fester and grow, Absalom finally had his brother murdered in retaliation for the rape. Absalom then fled for his own life, and for years the family's unity and happiness was destroyed.

In Genesis 34, a woman named Dinah was seized and raped by a Gentile prince. His act embittered the members of the Hebrew tribe, who initiated their revenge by saying to the Gentiles, "Only on this condition will we consent to you: that you will become as we are and every male among you be circumcised. Then we will give our daughters to you." (Genesis 34:15-16a). The prince's men agreed to be circumcised. While the Gentiles were recuperating, the Hebrews made a surprise attack, killed the entire tribe, and took all of the women captive. The Hebrews believed that the rape justified this retaliation.

Today, people are still subject to sexual violence, and society continues to have difficulty dealing with the problem. Considered the most serious sexual offense covered by the criminal law, rape is one of the crimes that frequently carries the death penalty. Yet in many instances, people convicted of rape do not receive stiff penalties. An overburdened legal system, overcrowding in prisons, and the difficulty in making convictions when the victim is the only witness are three of the factors that may explain this inequity in punishments. However, we may also need to give thought to our society's attitudes toward women and sex in general and toward rape in particular—attitudes that may contribute to such inequity.

Psychologists and sociologists have begun to categorize rapes. Separate categories exist for rape by strangers, rape by acquaintances, rape by physical violence or the threat of violence, rape based on position of authority, rape by seduction of children too young to be responsible for their actions, gang rapes, and rape during a date. While different types of rape may cause different emotions in the victims and may be viewed in different ways by society, they are all violent acts of sex committed against the will of the victim.

Date rape is one category of rape that is often difficult to prove, but like all other categories, it is illegal. Our sons and daughters need to be aware of the threat of date rape. We must teach our youth to act responsibly when dating and must stress to them that the dating relationship does not give one person the right to impose his or her will upon another. Parents need to make sure their children know that laws stand behind their right to say no and that they have a right to protect themselves against this kind of attack.

Nearly half of all rape victims seen in hospital emergency rooms are under 18, and 15 percent are under 12. Rape is not just an issue for adult men and women—it affects our children. Perhaps one important thing that parents can do about rape is to encourage our children to treat women as equals. We need to teach our sons that women are not objects to be victimized when a man wishes to display his power.

VIOLENT WORDS

In reality, only a small percentage of people exert power over others in the form of actual rape. But many people commit a more subtle form of sexual violence by using sexual words as a means of aggression. People use sex-related slang words as a tool for hurting or insulting others, especially as a means for expressing anger. The words give the speaker the illusion of control. With them, the speaker not only devalues another person but also symbolically violates that person. Sexual gestures become a way to indicate power without having to prove it and also serve as a way of saying, "You can't hurt me because I don't respect you."

When people use sexual innuendo in their jokes, they may be capitalizing on the shock value of mentioning traditional taboos. The humor often comes because people feel uncomfortable or embarrassed with body parts, functions, or even odors, yet want to pretend that they are not. Off-color jokes tend to perpetuate sexual stereotypes, including the idea that women are sex objects.

How should parents handle it when their children come home with dirty words or undesirable jokes? In our family, we tell the children that there are some words that are not acceptable. Even if we have seen them displayed in public places or heard them on television or in the movies, it is probably not wise to use them. We ask our children if they know the real meaning of the word or understand the joke (often they don't), and then we discuss why people would say that. We suggest that it is usually best to avoid using words in conversation if we don't know their meaning. We talk about how children and adults sometimes use unac-

88

ceptable words to impress others, but that such speech is often a sign of immaturity instead. We don't condemn anyone for using this language, but try not to use such words ourselves and suggest that there are usually more positive word choices. We stress that our words should be affirming and uplifting, not ways of putting people down. If children feel sad because someone has called them a dirty name, we talk about the fact that words can't change the value of who we are inside.

The glossary at the conclusion of this book includes some street terms, slang expressions, and euphemisms after the definition of the appropriate word. Although some persons may find the inclusion of these words offensive, we believe that it is essential for parents to be equipped to handle a child's question about words they encounter written on the walls of a public restroom, spoken in a movie, or printed in a book. We have not included these words because we support their use, but specifically because we too find them inappropriate, offensive, and often hate-filled and demeaning.

SEX IN THE MEDIA

It is hard to underestimate the role modern media plays in shaping and identifying our values. Almost every American home has at least one television set, and many family members spend 30 hours or more per week watching it. Television has become a cultural institution of our time—what is seen on TV serves as the standard for judging the quality and reality of life. It suggests how we should think, what we should value, and how we should look and behave. If a person's impression of life does not fit the image portrayed by TV, the television is often viewed as the one to trust.

Television programming makes strong statements about sexuality. A majority of primary characters are white, unmarried, middle-class males. These men are powerful and often violent. Women are slender, beautiful, and usually dressed in expensive clothes. Intimate sexual interactions are shown or alluded to several times per hour during prime time, with intercourse between unmarried persons shown several times more frequently than intercourse between married couples. Single women are frequently pictured as less mature or capable than married women, and prostitution and rape are common themes. Cable television has brought R-rated movies and sexually explicit music videos into the home. The soaps seem to glamorize adultery and divorce.

The commercials on television and in magazines also make claims about the shape sexuality should take. Items are advertised as having the ability to make buyers more desirable, and brand names are portrayed as status symbols. Sex is used to sell products, and even the packaging of a product can be sexually suggestive. Commercials tend to perpetuate stereotypes about appropriate behavior for men and women, with women pictured in ads for household cleaners, baby products, and beauty items, but men speaking as the voice of authority for most other items. Commercials tend to convey the view that attractive adults are young. Few advertisements—except for medical products or insurance—show people who are over 50.

Although the portrayal of sexuality in the media may be offensive to some people, its portrayal of violence is even more disturbing. Topping the list of America's favorite actors are "human action figures." Theatrical wrestling programs glorify hatred, revenge, and violence, even breaking so-called "rules" in the process. Children watching TV see their favorite characters settling disagreements with fistfights and handguns; high-speed car chases and murders are regular features in many scripts. Many shows and movies depict men using force on women, with the women frequently appearing to enjoy this force.

Researchers have found that children watching violence on TV are more likely to participate in violent behavior themselves. They have also found that men who are exposed to sexually violent movies appear to display a higher degree of aggression towards women. Desensitized by watching scenes of explicit violence against women, both men and women appear to become less sympathetic toward injured or sexually assaulted persons in real life.

On the other hand, research has also found that heavy exposure to non-violent but sexually explicit movies results in a sharp decrease in aggressive behaviors, not the increase that most people fear. Apparently, persons who view high amounts of sex-related films become bored, rather than excited, by what they see.

Most children watch large amounts of TV, often in the absence of an adult. Parents need to be aware of the message their children are receiving in their viewing and have a strong obligation to guide their children's TV-watching habits. We have the right to say, "I don't want you watching that; I don't want you to think it is okay for people to hurt one another that way." We also have the opportunity to watch TV or movies with our children and to discuss together the values and attitudes that we see. We can use television as the starting point for talking about sex. Or we can say, "Let's do something instead of watching TV tonight!" We can make sure our children have access to other information and viewpoints besides those typically portrayed on TV.

HOMOSEXUALITY

Homosexuality is a difficult and sometimes painful reality of American society. Many people fear, misunderstand, and even hate people who have a sexual preference for persons of their own sex, and these people use verses such as Leviticus 20:13 ("If a man lies with a male as with a woman, both of them have committed an abomination") to emphasize their disapproval. Although rarely enforced, laws banning "crimes against nature"—which include male homosexual activities—remain on the books in many states. Socially ostracized and the victims of discrimination, many homosexuals feel the need to conceal their sexual orientation.

Researchers are not yet able to pinpoint or agree upon the cause(s) of homosexuality, but the American Psychiatric Association has removed it from the category of mental illness. Most child development specialists assure parents that childhood homosexual curiosity and sex play do not indicate, determine, or alter basic sexual orientation. A single experience with homosexual behavior does not mean that a person is a homosexual.

No matter what our personal opinion concerning the morality of homosexuality may be, there are some things we can do as parents in relationship to this issue. First of all, we can raise our children to be loving and kind to all persons, and we can help them to treat everyone with dignity and respect. Second, we can teach our children to avoid judging others on the basis of mannerisms, body build, and speech. We can help them to realize that not all homosexuals are alike, just as not all heterosexuals are alike. We can also dispel current myths, such as the idea that most molesters are male homosexuals when, in fact, over 90 percent of the sexual offenses against children are heterosexual men who victimize girls. Third, we can assure our children that we will always be there for them, that we will never reject them, and that they can feel free to talk with us about their concerns and feelings.

SEXUALLY TRANSMITTED DISEASES

Although sexuality is a very private matter, our sexual activity cannot be viewed as exclusively our own business. More than twelve million persons (three million of whom are teenagers) are known to be infected by Sexually Transmitted Diseases (STDs) each year. Many of these diseases can cause serious bodily injury and even death. The Sexuality Information & Education Council of the United States (SIECUS) estimates that as many as 56 million persons have an incurable viral STD other than HIV. Nearly 72,000 of those 12 million persons are victims of AIDS (Acquired Immune Deficiency Syndrome), which can be sexually transmitted and currently has no cure. Estimates of unreported cases push these numbers much higher.

One-fifth of all AIDS patients and over one-half of the persons with other STDs are under 25 years old. SIECUS reports that by the end of 1995, an estimated 2,300 teenagers had been diagnosed with AIDS. We cannot afford to raise youth who are ignorant of the causes and seriousness of these diseases. We have a responsibility to warn our children and to teach them how to keep themselves safe.

The term "safe sex" was coined by the New York Task Force on AIDS. It refers to reasonable ways for protecting ourselves against disease and for keeping from knowingly spreading disease to others. Safe sex means taking precautions: avoid intercourse with someone who is infected; avoid promiscuous or group sex; avoid sex with high-risk individuals (such as intravenous drug users); use condoms and spermicides to reduce the risk of infection; take a shower, using warm water and soap, immediately after having sexual intercourse; be honest about your past sexual behavior; secure medical attention immediately if you suspect that you have contracted an infection; and inform your partner if you are carrying a disease. Sex is safest in relationships where neither person has had intercourse with a different partner.

Parents should be aware that three million teens contract a sexually transmitted disease each year, according to SIECUS. Most of the diseases (with the exception of AIDS) are readily treated with antibiotics. Yet many youth, particularly those in states that require adult permission before a teenager may receive treatment, do not secure medical attention. Our children need to be assured that we value their health and that

92

we will provide prompt medical care and support, even if we do not condone their sexual activity.

AIDS. Acquired Immune Deficiency Syndrome is an illness that weakens a person's immune system so that the body cannot fight off infections and certain cancers. Two diseases commonly associated with AIDS are a cancer called Kaposi's sarcoma and a type of pneumonia called Pneumoceptis Carnii.

The virus that causes AIDS is the Human Immunodeficiency Virus (HIV). Most people infected with HIV have no symptoms, although they may experience an enlargement of their lymph nodes, fever, diarrhea, and weight loss. Since it can take years for AIDS to develop, it has not yet been determined if everyone with this virus will get AIDS. HIV is found in body fluids such as semen, blood, cervical secretions, and occasionally in the saliva of infected persons. It enters the bloodstream through cuts in the skin or mucous membranes.

AIDS is transmitted by sexual contact with a person who has the AIDS virus or by sharing needles with an infected person during intravenous drug abuse. Pregnant women who have AIDS may give the virus to their babies. HIV has been transmitted in the past through blood transfusions, but blood banks in the United States have all but eliminated this risk by screening donors and by testing all donated blood for the presence of HIV antibodies. AIDS is not transmitted by casual contact. A person cannot pick up the virus from toilet seats, swimming pools, doorknobs, or drinking cups. There is no evidence that mosquitoes or pets other than chimpanzees can carry the disease.

Through massive research efforts and education, the mortality rate from AIDS has dropped somewhat. One estimate suggests a 47 percent decline in AIDS-related deaths. Still, AIDS remains a major worldwide health concern.

In the United States, male homosexuals have had the highest rate of infection, followed by intravenous drug abusers. It is also possible to contract AIDS through heterosexual contacts. In some countries there are more heterosexuals than homosexuals with AIDS. The disease is rare among children, although 571 cases in children under 13 were reported in the United States by September 1987.[3]

Children can be protected from getting diseases such as AIDS by being taught never to pick up hypodermic needles that they see lying around, never to use intravenous drugs, and never to participate in "blood brother or sister ceremonies" by cutting or pricking their fingers and sharing their blood. They should be taught to say "No" if a grown-up wants to touch the private parts of their bodies.

Older children should be taught that the best way to be safe from AIDS is to avoid risky behavior. Affirm their decisions not to become sexually active and not to use illicit drugs. All youth need to know, however, that they should use condoms if they decide to become sexually active and that they should avoid sexual practices that could damage body tissues (such as anal intercourse).

There is currently no cure for AIDS. Experimental drugs are being tested with some success. Scientists are also attempting to develop a vaccine against the AIDS virus, but have not yet been successful.

Recent interviews with women on college campuses have found that many girls do not want to offend their partner by asking him to wear a condom. It appears that they find it easier to risk the possibility of catching a deadly disease than to risk the displeasure of a male. Parents must teach both their sons and daughters that they can stand up for themselves without embarrassment. We must teach our children to be assertive and to have a strong self-esteem that values self-preservation over the approval of someone else. We must also teach our children that selfishness and pride are no reasons to endanger the life of another person.

Gonorrhea. Gonorrhea is an STD that has been known for thousands of years. The term was used as early as 140 B.C.

Gonorrhea is caused by tiny bacteria that cannot survive outside the human body for more than a few seconds. The first symptoms appear three to five days following sexual contact with an infected person. Symptoms include a discharge from the penis or vagina; an extremely painful, burning sensation during urination; and redness, inflammation, and irritation in the genital area.

Untreated gonorrhea can spread through the reproductive system and cause sterility, can enter the bloodstream, and spread to the spine, joints, or heart. Blindness can be caused if the bacteria come into contact with the eye. The silver nitrate solution put into the eyes of newborns after birth is to prevent this disease from being passed from an infected

94

mother to her baby during childbirth. Gonorrhea can usually be treated with large doses of penicillin.

Syphilis. In the early stages of the disease, syphilis bacteria cause skin lesions at the point of contact—the external sex organs, the vagina, urethra, anus, mouth, or breasts. During the second stage of the disease, the person may develop a rash, high fever, severe headaches, sore throat, and loss of hair. Eventually, from two to twenty-five years after the infection, the bacteria may attack almost any organ of the body and form lesions in the bones, joints, eyes, mouth, and throat. Persons who are not treated may experience loss of muscle control, paralysis, blindness, deafness, heart disease, or insanity, and may even die.

Congenital syphilis can be transferred from an infected pregnant woman to her baby, causing death or birth defects. Many states have laws that require testing for syphilis before a couple can obtain a marriage license, or during the early months of pregnancy.

Penicillin is virtually 100 percent effective as a treatment for syphilis, especially if taken within one to two hours after contact. Cloretetracycline and Oxtetracycline are also effective.

Genital Herpes (Herpes Simplex Type II). Another sexually transmitted disease is Genital Herpes. Caused by a virus that remains for life in the body of the individual, this disease causes tiny blisters in the genital area. Women with herpes are more susceptible to cervical cancer, and the disease can cause severe brain damage and death to babies. No cure has yet been found, although the drug Acyclovir shortens the period of infection.

Chlamydia. Chlamydia trachomatis is the most prevalent of all sexually transmitted diseases, with an estimated four million reported cases each year. If untreated, chlamydia can cause genital and pelvic infections, miscarriage, and infertility. Pregnant women with chlamydia can infect their babies during the delivery process. Nearly five times more women than men are reported to have this disease, and infection rates are highest among teenagers and young adults. While some other STDs have shown a decline over the past decade, reported cases of chlamydia are on the rise. Yet fewer than 25 percent of American adults cite chlamydia when asked to name a sexually transmitted disease. Chlamydia can be treated with antibiotics.

Trichomoniasis. Trichomoniasis is an infection that causes vaginal discharge and irritation, and may infect the urethra, bladder, and Bartholin glands. As many as one fourth of all gynecological patients in the United States have this infection. Males can also be infected, although they usually develop little discomfort from the disease. Trichomoniasis can be transmitted by sexual intercourse, as well as by bath water or unchlorinated swimming pools, or by sharing towels. The infection can be treated with Metronidazole.

UNPLANNED PREGNANCIES

Sexual intercourse can have other consequences besides the chance of catching a disease. The most obvious, of course, is pregnancy. Some teenage pregnancies are accidents, some are not. Many adolescents lack a clear understanding of the emotional and economic effects of pregnancy and parenthood. According to statistics by the Alan Guttmacher Institute in 1981, there were nearly 1.25 million teenage pregnancies in the United States each year. A 1996 report from the institute says the number has declined slightly, but the U.S. teen pregnancy rate is still twice that of England, Wales, and Canada. Many young women are sexually active, yet nationwide surveys have consistently found that half or more of these girls use contraceptives only occasionally or not at all. Some girls admit their belief that they could not become pregnant the first time they had intercourse.

There are approximately a half a million babies born to teenage mothers every year. That's nearly 13 percent of all live births in the United States! There are risks to both the mother and the baby when the mother is young. Babies of teenage mothers tend to have a lower birth weight. They are generally weaker, more susceptible to health problems, and may have improperly developed organs and mental disabilities. Teenage mothers tend to have more difficult deliveries and a higher rate of death due to childbirth complications.

Many of these families are living in poverty or are on welfare. Both unwed mothers and teens who decide to marry have difficulty finishing their schooling and obtaining sufficient funds to provide for their children. Two out of every three pregnant teenagers drop out of school. The divorce rate for couples who marry during their teens is very high. Parents need to encourage their sons and daughters to think before engaging in sexual activity. Have they thought through the possible consequences? What plans have they made for birth control? What do they intend to do if pregnancy occurs? Will they get married? Put the child up for adoption? Have an abortion? Will the mother try to raise the baby on her own, or expect her parents to help? Are they aware of the costs of raising a baby or the time and attention that young children

96

require and deserve? Would they be willing to sacrifice their education and their dreams, if necessary, for the sake of a child?

Obviously a teenager will not stop to answer all of these questions when he or she is caught up in a moment of sexual excitement. That is why it is important to talk about these kinds of questions early. Even older grade school children can think seriously about the consequences of pregnancy, although they may not be able to understand the emotional aspects that would be involved. If they have been encouraged to think about the subject while they are still young, they will hopefully continue to think when they are older.

One way to encourage children to think about sexual matters might be when you are talking about other people. Are there students in your neighborhood who are pregnant? Do you know a boy who is thinking about dropping out of school? Do you know someone who has recently adopted an infant? Is there a relative in your family who "had to get married"? Talking over other people's predicaments can be an opportunity to think through your values and plan how to avoid similar circumstances.

SPECIAL NEEDS AND PROBLEMS OF EXCEPTIONAL CHILDREN

The parents of exceptional children need to remember that their son or daughter is also a sexual being, just like every other boy or girl. Mental and physical disabilities do not rule out sexual feelings. The need for touch, warmth, tenderness, and intimacy remains, as does the need for sex education. Assure children with disabilities that their bodies are okay. Persons with intellectual disabilities may function at a childlike level, but have adult sexual desires. Here are a few resources that may be helpful:

Sexuality and People with Intellectual Disability, by Lydia Fegen, Anne Rauch, and Wendy McCarthy (Paul H. Brooks Publishing, Baltimore, Maryland), is a book that takes a frank look at sexuality and examines the underlying attitudes of both the person and his or her caregivers. Included in the text are some sample dialogues and a discussion on the sexual rights of people with intellectual disabilities.

An Easy Guide For Parents: Sexuality and Socialization, by Lynn McKee and Virginia Blacklidge (Planned Parenthood/Shasta Diablo, Concord,

California) is a helpful guide for those wishing to understand the social needs of children with intellectual disabilities. Sexual development is discussed, focusing on items such as responsible sexual behavior, masturbation, sexual abuse, birth control, and marriage.

LIKE A DEER PRANCING INTO A TRAP

Proverbs 7 tells the colorful story of an inexperienced and foolish young man who was not aware of the difficult sexual situations that exist in the world. Naive and unprepared, he was easily seduced by a beautiful but shameless woman.

> *She seizes him and kisses him, and with impudent face she says to him: ". . . Come, let us take our fill of love until morning; let us delight ourselves with love." . . . Right away he follows her, and goes like an ox to the slaughter, or bounds like a stag toward the trap . . . He is like a bird rushing into a snare, not knowing that it will cost him his life.*
> *(Proverbs 7:13, 18, 22, 23b)*

The world in which our children live is a world of potential sexual danger. Children may be walking nonchalantly through life, only to be thrown off guard by sexual abuse, rape, AIDS, or an unplanned pregnancy. A problem like that could be devastating—even life-destroying! We must be purposeful about preparing our children for life. As parents, we have a responsibility to see that our children are informed, aware, and able to protect themselves. Life will always have dangers, but if our children are prepared, they will be able to cope and to keep a positive perspective on what it means to be male or female.

WHAT CAUSED THE PROBLEM?

It is hard to ignore the list of difficulties associated with human sexuality. What causes sex-related problems? Throughout history, it seems people have either idealized or ignored sexuality as a part of life. We have either so flaunted sexuality that it lost all of its mystery or so covered it up that all of its beauty was hidden in guilt.

Early Greek and Roman philosophers viewed sexual desire as irrational and immature. This made it difficult for a person who felt sexual urges to achieve both pleasure and self-respect. Women in particular were not supposed to enjoy sex. Couples did not marry for love, but for the purpose of having children. These attitudes were magnified in doctrines of the early Christian church, in which the leaders wrote that to enjoy sex was sinful, even within marriage. In the Middle Ages, "courtly love" became the fashion. Courtly love was tender and passionate, but not consummated with sexual intercourse. It was thought to make lovers noble, and had no association with marriage. Marriages then, as in many parts of the world today, were arranged by parents on the basis of economic necessity or social standing.

Early Hebrew laws instructed women to "purify" themselves after their menstrual period and after childbirth, so even these natural occurrences could leave a feeling of having done something wrong. Procreation was seen as an obligation, so if a couple did not produce a child, they were failing to fulfill their duty. When a person was infertile or too old to bear children, he or she was believed to be under God's curse, and had no right to sexual pleasure. It could be life-threatening for a Hebrew person to engage in improper sexual behavior. Women caught in the act of adultery were stoned to death. Genesis 38:8-10 tells how a man named Onan was put to death for engaging in coitus interruptus (withdrawing the penis before ejaculation).

This is probably one reason why the Old Testament characters were so concerned and upset with the sinfulness of their neighbors. The Hebrews wanted to raise their children to fear Yahweh and to obey God's commandments and to be faithful to their heritage and customs as a people. Their desire for their sons and daughters to grow up and marry other Hebrews was central to their survival as a people. However, the Egyptians who held them as slaves, the tribes they encountered while wandering in the wilderness, and the Assyrians and Babylonians who carried them into exile, all held different attitudes about sexuality. This was particularly true of the resident tribes with whom they reluctantly shared Palestine. Deeply ingrained into these religions was a worship of idols that carried sexual implications and ritual prostitution.

Apparently these sexual practices proved to be a powerful recruitment tool, used by the people of Canaan in an attempt to draw the Hebrews to the worship of idols. Parents and prophets in Old Testament times continually had to warn the younger generation against being seduced by or adopting the values and practices of these other cultures and religions.

During the Victorian era in England (1837-1910), anything with even a remote association to sex could not be discussed. A person could not talk about eating a "breast" of chicken—you had to call it "white meat." Piano and table legs were covered with fabric to discourage the sexual excitement one might feel in response to looking at the furniture! People began eating "anti-aphrodisiacs" to suppress sexual impulse. For example, Sylvester Graham invented graham crackers, claiming that the wholesomeness of this food would reduce sexual desire.

Some Christian sects perpetuated the belief that sex was somehow shameful. The Shakers' vow of celibacy, even within marriage, caused them to eventually die out, leaving only their writings and some exquisite furniture to remember them by! Several churches built separate entrances for men and women. Interpretations of references by Paul to "the flesh" as sinful have confused many a Christian as they have sought to reconcile body and soul.

Today many Christian parents realize that their particular values about sex are not reflected in popular culture. Our faith, not just our culture, informs the way we feel about homosexuality, abortion, premarital sex, and promiscuity. Hopefully, it also informs our views on healthy relationships, passion, and positive sexual expression. But youth place great emphasis on the viewpoints and ideals of their friends and heroes. For example, our youth may face tremendous peer pressure to engage in premarital sex, even in their early teens. Television commercials appear to indicate that persons need only buy a car or switch brands of toothpaste or deodorant in order to become sexually appealing. It is obvious that the sexual attitudes and actions of many movie stars, celebrated athletes, or popular musicians do not represent the sexual expression we wish for our children.

PART OF SEX EDUCATION IS LEARNING TO LOVE

Our family subscribes to cable television, and we enjoy watching movies together. Of course, it is almost impossible to find movies that don't make some kind of reference to sex. When our children were younger (and sometimes even still), they used to play the role of "sexuality censors" for these movies. "Yuk! They're kissing! Close your eyes!" they would demand. Laughing, they would scrunch their eyes shut and try to cover our eyes with their hands, knocking our glasses into the bridge of our noses. It became a kind of game.

But sometimes when there would be a bedroom scene, we would catch the kids peeking at the screen out of the corner of their eyes. "What are they doing?" they would ask. We would tend to say something like, "They are showing that they love one another."

It has become common to call sexual intercourse "making love," even though in some cases the act has little to do with love. The desire for sexual intercourse does not bond persons together unless that desire is coupled with genuine caring and affection. While we realize that sexual experiences are not always expressions of love, we still believe that love is the ideal. To us, one of the purposes of sex education is learning how to integrate love and sexuality. As the world-famous psychoanalyst, Dr. Erich Fromm, says in his book, *The Art of Loving*, it is the experience of love that lifts a person from feelings of isolation and aloneness: "Sexual attraction creates, for the moment, the illusion of union, yet without love this union leaves strangers as far apart as they were before."[4]

The seventeenth century Puritans were among the first to view sex as a positive bond of pleasure, a gift from God intended to strengthen and enhance marriage. As contemporary Christians, we believe this viewpoint is still valuable and valid and one which we uphold for our children. We want our children to see how actions of love can be beautiful and appropriate ways to express concern and care for another person. As Fromm says, "What does one person give to another?"

> *He gives of himself, of the most precious he has, he gives of his life. This does not necessarily mean that he sacrifices his life for the other, but that he gives . . . that which is alive in him: he gives . . . of his joy, of his interest, of his understanding, of his knowledge, of his humor, of his sadness—of all expressions and manifestations of that which is alive in him.[5]*

SEXUALITY AS AN EXPRESSION OF GOD'S DESIRE FOR HUMANITY

One of the fundamentals of our Christian faith is that we ought to love one another. The ability and desire to care for others is both a gift and a command:

Beloved, let us love one another, because love is from God;
everyone who loves is born of God and knows God. . . . God is
love, and those who abide in love abide in God, and God abides
in them. Love has been perfected among us in this. . . . There is
no fear in love, but perfect love casts out fear.
(1 John 4:7, 16b-17a, 18a)

We were created in the image of God. Genesis 1:27 says that in giving birth to us, God formed a being that is incomplete on its own—a being that needs the touch and warmth of companionship in order to reach its full human potential. To be human is to need relationship and love. Babies need to be held and cuddled in order to thrive. Older adults who are isolated from human contact become depressed, lose touch with reality, and no longer exhibit the will to live. At every age, our yearning to be close to other persons is an expression of our basic need for relationship.

One of the key components of this yearning is our sexuality. Though by gender we are either male or female, we each have a unique interpretation of what it means to be male and what it means to be female. We have individual ways of expressing maleness and femaleness. Yet despite these interpretations and expressions, the role of sexuality remains the same. Our sexuality is both a symbol and a power. As a symbol it reminds us of our need for others in becoming what God has imagined for us. Created in the image of God, we too are creators—creators of beauty, of relationships, and of new life. As a power, our sexuality draws us ever more deeply into the intimacy where we discover our creative potential and that of our sisters and brothers.

Affirming and expressing our God-given sexuality is a way to understand the indwelling presence of God in our lives. Ours is a passionate God who weeps when estranged, who continues to seek after us, who came to us in the birth of Christ, and who comes to us in the act of Communion as a God of the flesh as well as of the spirit. God enters into our lives in a real and human way, calling us to accept the touch and power of God's love and longing to fill our emptiness and make us whole.

God's desire for humanity is that we should not be separated from God nor from others, for alienation from God and others is life-denying and destructive. Unfortunately, we know that sex can be a vehicle for alienation when it is used to dominate or to limit another, to express hostility, or to cause pain and fear. But this alienation is a result of sexuality misused, of sex used to manipulate and bruise. This kind of sex is aggressive; it kills and destroys not only self-esteem, but also the spirit that binds us into relationships. God came to us in bodily form that we "may have life, and have it abundantly" (John 10:10). Such a life is accepting of self and affirming of others and recognizes the God-given element of sexuality. It will not be expressed in oppression or dominance, but in vulnerability, openness, and respect. As such, it can be a vehicle for wholeness and joy. It is our great privilege as parents to assist our children in the discovery of such a life.

A PRAYER FOR PARENTS AND CHILDREN LIVING IN AN IMPERFECT WORLD

Loving God,
We live in a confusing and dangerous world—

—a world where children are sexually abused, sometimes by the very ones who ought to love them the most;

—a world where the words and acts of intimacy can be distorted into weapons of violence and power;

—a world where children have children, where TV speaks louder than the heart, and where people risk death or disease for a moment of pleasure. Forgive us, Lord.

Help us to make our world a place of safety, and teach us to embrace sexuality as a source and force of love!

Amen.

ENDNOTES

Chapter 3:

1. John Money, *Love and Love Sickness: The Science of Sex, Gender Difference and Pair Bonding*, Baltimore: Johns Hopkins University Press, 1980.
2. M. Ainsworth, M.L. Blehar, E. Waters and S. Wall. *Patterns of Attachment*, Hissdale, New Jersey: Erlbaum, 1978.
3. M. Louise Biggar, "Maternal Aversion to Mother-Infant Contact," *The Many Facets of Touch, The Foundation of Experience: Its Importance Through Life, With Initial Emphasis for Infants and Young Children*, Johnson and Johnson, 1984, pp. 66-74.
4. Anneliese Korner, "The Many Faces of Touch," *The Many Facets of Touch*, Johnson and Johnson, 1984, pp. 107-113.
5. E.H. Erikson, *Childhood and Society*, 2nd Edition, New York: Norton, 1963.
6. E.E. Maccoby and C.N. Jacklin. *The Psychology of Sex Difference*, Standford, California: Standford University Press, 1974.
7. L. Shapio, "A Study of Peer Groups Interaction in 8 and 28 Month Old Children," Ph.D. Dissertation, Harvard University, 1969.
8. J.W.M. Whiting and B. Whiting, cited in W. Mischel's "Sex Stereotyping and Socialization," *Carmichael's Manual of Child Psychology*, Vol. 2, 3rd Ed., New York: Wiley, 1970.
9. Sandra Weiss, "The Language of Touch: A Resource to Body Image," Issues in Mental Health Nursing, Vol. 1, 1978, pp. 17-29.

Chapter 4:

1. Susan M. Bennett, "Family Environment for Sexual Learning as a Function of Father's Involvement in Family Work and Discipline," *Adolescence,* Vol. XIX, No. 75, Fall, 1984, pp. 609-627.

Chapter 5:

1. Paul C. Vance, "Love and Sex—Can We Talk About That at School?", *Childhood Education*, Vol. 61, No. 4, March/April 1985, pp. 272-276.
2. Patricia Beezley Mrazek and C. Haney Kempe. *Sexually Abused Children and Their Families*, New York: Pergamon Press, 1981, pp. 91-92, 230.
3. U.S. Department of Health and Human Services, Public Health Service. Centers for Disease Control.
4. Erich Fromm, The Art of Loving, New York: Harper and Row, 1956, p. 46.
5. Erich Fromm, op. cit., p. 20.

GLOSSARY

Included in parentheses after the following definitions are some of the street terms, slang expressions, and euphemisms commonly used in reference to human anatomy and sexual behaviors. We find the use of many such expressions offensive and demeaning, especially when terms related to sexual intercourse double as ways of speaking about acts of violence or are used to verbally abuse others. The words included are ones your children will encounter on the street, at school, on television, in movies, or on the walls of public restrooms. Adults who understand the meaning of these words can direct their children to proper terminology and can help their children adopt a more Godly, loving attitude toward sex and sexuality. There is also a self-esteem issue raised: Children will feel better about themselves if they know what words mean—even words that they have no intention of using.

abortion. The surgical removal of an embryo or fetus from a pregnant woman's uterus before the embryo or fetus is able to survive on its own.

Acquired Immune Deficiency Syndrome (AIDS). A disease caused by the Human Immunodeficiency Virus (HIV). AIDS causes the breakdown of the body's immune system, making it impossible for the body to fight off other diseases. AIDS is transmitted by the exchange of body fluids—primarily through sexual intercourse, but also through the sharing of needles by drug users and from infected mothers to their babies.

adolescence. The period of life extended from the beginning of puberty to adulthood.

amniocentesis (AM-nee-oh-sen-TEE-sis). The surgical insertion of a hollow needle through a woman's abdominal wall and into the uterus to obtain a sample of the amniotic fluid. This process is used to check for birth defects in a developing fetus.

amnion (AM-nee-ahn). The thin membrane sac filled with a watery solution called amniotic fluid that surrounds and protects the developing fetus in its mother's uterus.

ampulla (am-POOL-uh). The flared-out portion of the vas deferens near the prostate gland, where sperm are stored until ejaculated.

androgen. A hormone that influences growth and the sex drive in males. It is responsible for sex characteristics such as voice change and hair growth.

anus. The opening in the rectum for the expulsion of solid waste—feces—from the body. (asshole)

artificial insemination. The introduction of semen into the vagina of a woman by means other than sexual intercourse in an attempt to overcome fertility problems.

athletic supporter. An elastic strap worn around the pelvic area by men and boys during strenuous exercise. Supports and protects the testicles by holding them close to the body. Commonly known as a jock strap.

bartholin glands. Two small, oval-shaped glands in the female that produce a lubricating fluid in the vaginal area.

Basal Body Temperature (BBT). A technique for determining female ovulation by observing changes in body temperature upon awakening each morning.

birth control. Preventing conception from taking place.

birth control pill. A medication that prevents ovulation and therefore prevents pregnancy. Medication must be taken exactly as prescribed in order to be effective. Often referred to as the pill.

bisexuality. Being sexually active with or sexually attracted to both sexes. (AC/DC, bi, swings both ways)

breasts. Two glands on the upper chest of both males and females, the growth of which is stimulated at puberty. In females, the breasts develop so that they are able to produce milk at the birth of a baby. (boobs, jugs, hooters, knockers, melons, tits)

caesarean section. Delivery of a baby by surgical incision through the abdomen into the uterus.

cervix (SIR-viks). The lower, narrow portion of the uterus that connects with the vagina.

chancre (SHANG-kuhr). A sore or ulcerated area, usually on the genitals, that appears during the early stage of syphilis.

chlamydia (KLUH-MID-ee-uh). A bacteria-caused STD that is a particular problem for females because of the lack of external symptoms. A

106

woman can appear healthy while the disease is spreading infection and seriously damaging the uterus, fallopian tubes, and ovaries.

chromosome. The DNA-containing structure in the nucleus of a cell that serves as the carrier of genes and genetic information.

circumcision. The surgical removal of the foreskin—the loose layer of skin that extends off the glans or head of the penis—for hygienic, religious, or cosmetic reasons.

clitoris (KLIT-uh-ris). The small, cylinder-shaped, highly sensitive female organ located at the top of the inner labia. It corresponds to the penis in males. (button, clit, pea)

conceive. To become pregnant.

conception. The fertilization of the female ovum by the male sperm, which marks the beginning of pregnancy.

condom. A thin sheath, usually of rubber or latex, placed on the erect penis before sexual intercourse to prevent the spread of disease and/or to prevent sperm from entering the vagina. Also called a prophylactic. (rubber, safe, protection)

cunnilingus (kuhn-uh-LING-guhs). Using the mouth to stimulate the vulva and vagina. (eating)

diaphragm. A soft rubber dome that is filled with a spermicide and inserted into the vagina before sexual intercourse.

douche. The cleansing of the vagina with a liquid solution or water.

ejaculation. The discharge of semen from the penis in a series of intense muscle contractions during orgasm. (come)

embryo. An unborn human from about the tenth day after conception until the third month of pregnancy.

endometrium (ehn-doh-MEE-tree-uhm). The uterine lining that thickens and fills with blood in preparation to receive a fertilized ovum.

epididymis (ep-uh-DID-uh-mihs). The mass of tiny tubes where sperm cells mature. It is attached to the back portion of the testicle.

erection. The enlargement and hardening of the penis or clitoris as tissues fill with blood, usually in response to sexual stimulation. (males— boner, hard-on, woody)

erogenous (ih-RAHG-uh-nuhs) zones. Areas of the body that are especially sensitive to sexual stimulation, including the mouth, lips, breasts, nipples, anus, and genitals.

estrogen. The female sex hormone that is produced primarily in the ovaries and is responsible for the development of secondary sex characteristics such as breast development and widened hips.

fallopian (fa-LOH-pee-unh) tubes. The two tubes through which the ova pass from the ovaries to the uterus.

fellatio (ful-LAY-she-oh). Oral stimulation of the penis. (blow job, hummer, sucking off, head job)

fertility. The condition of being able to produce offspring.

fertilization. The union of the sperm cell nucleus with the nucleus of the ovum to start a new baby. Also called conception.

fetus. An unborn human from about the third month of pregnancy until birth.

foreplay. Any type of sex play that precedes and prepares persons for sexual intercourse.

foreskin. The extension of loose skin that covers the glans or head of a male's penis at birth. Its removal for hygienic, religious, or cosmetic reasons is called circumcision.

gay. A homosexual person; more specifically, a male homosexual.

gender. Being male or female.

genital herpes (HER-peez). An incurable, virus-caused STD. In females it can lead to cancer of the cervix. The chief symptom is painful, blister-like sores that surface periodically for the remainder of the infected person's life.

genitals. The external male and female sex organs—the penis, scrotum, and testicles in males, and the vulva in females. (privates)

gestation. The period between conception and birth. Also called pregnancy.

gonads (GOH-nadz). The reproductive cell-producing glands; the testicles in the male and the ovaries in the female.

gonorrhea (gahn-uh-REE-uh). An STD caused by bacteria; can cause blindness, damage to heart and brain, severe arthritis, sterility, and death.

heterosexuality. Being sexually active or sexually attracted to a person or persons of the other sex. (hetero, straight)

homosexuality. Being sexually active with or sexually attracted to a person or persons of one's own sex. (female homosexual: dyke, les, lesbo, from "lesbian"; male homosexual: fag, faggot, fairy, fruit, homo, pansy, queen, queer)

hormones. Chemical substances, produced by glands, that regulate the functioning of other organs.

hymen (HI-muhn). A thin membrane that partially covers the opening to the vagina. It may be torn during strenuous exercise, masturbation, or first sexual intercourse. Some women are born without a hymen. (cherry, maidenhead)

hysterectomy (hiss-tuh-RECK-tuh-mee). Surgical removal of the uterus.

impotence (IHM-puh-tuhns). A male's inability to achieve or maintain an erection during sexual intercourse.

incest. Sexual intercourse between close relatives; a practice forbidden in most cultures.

intercourse. See sexual intercourse.

Intrauterine Device (IUD). A soft plastic or metal birth control device that must be inserted into and removed from the uterus by a doctor. While questions have been raised as to the safety of this means of birth control, it continues in use.

labia (LAY-bee-uh). Two sets of folds of skin that are part of the vulva. The outer or major labia surround the opening to the vagina. The inner or minor labia are inside and sometimes hidden by the outer labia. The word *labia* means "lips."

labor. The stage of giving birth during which the cervix dilates or enlarges, allowing the contractions of the uterine muscles to push the baby from the uterus into the vagina in preparation for delivery.

lesbian. A female homosexual.

masturbation (mass-tuhr-BAY-shuhn). Self-stimulation of one's genitals to create sexual pleasure. (beating off, beating the meat, getting your rocks off, jacking off, jerking off, playing with yourself, spanking the monkey, whacking off, pounding your pud)

menarche (muh-NAHR-kee). The onset of menstruation in females.

menopause (MEHN-uh-pahz). The time in a woman's life—usually between the ages of 45 and 55—during which menstruation ceases and pregnancy is no longer possible. Also referred to as change of life.

menstruation (mehn-STRAY-shun). The discharge of blood, secretions, and tissue from the uterus that females experience about once a month. Also referred to as the period.

miscarriage. The natural expulsion of an embryo or fetus from the uterus before it is mature enough to survive, usually due to some abnormal development. More properly referred to as a spontaneous abortion.

mons pubis (mahns PEW-bihs). The area at the base of the man's abdomen and just above the penis where the pubic bone is located. With the onset of puberty it is covered with hair.

mons veneris (mahns VEHN-uh-riss). The mound of fatty tissue covering the pubic bone at the base of the woman's abdomen, between the thighs. With the onset of puberty it is covered with hair. (bush, hair pie)

Natural Family Planning (NFP). Women wanting to avoid pregnancy keep charts of daily body temperature and cervical secretions in order to determine when ovulation is to take place. Intercourse is then avoided on certain days.

nocturnal emission. Spontaneous ejaculation of built-up semen that occurs during sleep and is often associated with sexual dreams. Also called a seminal emission or wet dream.

oral sex. Using the mouth to stimulate the genitals. (See fellatio, cunnilingus.)

orgasm. The peak of excitement in sexual activity, resulting in a highly pleasurable series of muscle spasms, and followed by a sudden discharge of accumulated sexual tension.

ovaries. Two almond-sized female reproductive glands in which ova develop and sex hormones are produced.

ovulation (ah-vue-LAY-shuhn). The ripening and release of an ovum from an ovary, usually occurring about once a month.

ovum. The female reproductive cell. The plural is ova.

penis. The cylindrical portion of the male genitals through which urine and semen pass. The primary parts are the shaft, glans or head, and foreskin. It corresponds to the clitoris in females. (cock, dick, meat, pecker, peter, prick, tool, wang, weiner)

period. The time of menstrual flow. (curse, on the rag, that time of the month)

petting. Noncoital sexual activity such as stimulation of the breasts and genitals. (feeling up)

pituitary (pih-TOO-uh-tar-ee) gland. An endocrine gland attached to the base of the brain that secretes a number of hormones to control body processes.

placenta (pluh-SEN-tuh). A spongy organ containing a network of blood vessels that develops on the lining of the uterus during pregnancy; it enables the exchange of food, oxygen, and waste materials between mother and child.

pregnancy. The period from conception to birth. The condition of having a developing embryo or fetus within the female body. (expecting, in a family way, knocked up)

prostate (PROSS-tate) gland. An organ surrounding the male urethra that secretes part of the seminal fluid. The contraction of the prostate helps to force the semen out through the urethra during ejaculation.

puberty (PEW-bur-tee). The period of rapid development during which the sex organs mature and begin to produce either ova or sperm.

pubic hair. Coarse, curly hair that grows in the genital area.

rape. Forcing someone to have sexual intercourse. (gang bang—rape by multiple assailants)

rectum. The lower end of the large intestine, ending at the anus.

sanitary napkin. A pad of absorbent cotton worn inside the underpants to absorb the menstrual discharge. (pad, rag)

scrotum. The loose pouch of skin in the male, beneath the penis, that contains the testicles. (bag, sack)

semen. The whitish fluid containing sperm, which is ejaculated from the penis during orgasm. Also called seminal fluid. (cum, jism)

seminal vesicles. Two small pouches in a male, located at the back of the prostate gland, where semen is produced.

sensuality. The unique combination of elements such as strength, vulnerability, sensitivity, honesty, self-esteem, energy level, and physical appearance that one person perceives and is attracted to in another person.

sex-role stereotypes. Culturally imposed, broad generalizations about particular traits associated with masculinity or femininity.

sexual intercourse. Sexual activity where the penis is inserted into the vagina. Also called coitus or copulation. (balling, banging, doing it, fucking, getting laid, going all the way, home run, making love, scoring, screwing, sleeping together)

sexuality. The sum of a person's sexual orientation, characteristics, and behaviors.

Sexually Transmitted Diseases (STDs). A variety of diseases contracted through sexual activity. These were formerly called venereal disease or VD.

sodomy (SAW-duh-mee). Anal intercourse. The term is also used at times in reference to oral sex or having sexual intercourse with an animal.

sperm. The male reproductive cell.

spermicide. A sperm-killing chemical placed in the vagina prior to sexual intercourse. It comes in the form of creams, jellies, dissolving tablets, and aerosol foams.

sterility. The inability to produce offspring. Also called infertility. (barren)

sterilization. The surgical procedure of making an individual permanently incapable of reproduction.

surrogate mother. A woman who is artificially inseminated by sperm from the male of a couple unable to conceive due to the female's infertility or inability to carry a child full term. The surrogate mother carries the child until birth and then gives the child to the couple.

syphilis (SIHF-uh-luhs). An STD caused by a microorganism called a spirochete; the first symptom appears 10-90 days or more after exposure in the form of a sore at the point where the infection entered the body. While the sore will eventually go away, the untreated disease can affect the brain, heart, liver, or bones, and can cause irreparable birth defects if passed from a mother to her unborn child.

tampon (TAM-pahn). A roll of absorbent material that is inserted into the vagina to absorb the menstrual discharge.

testicles (testes). The egg-shaped male reproductive glands in which sperm and testosterone are produced. They are suspended in a loose pouch of skin between the legs. (balls, family jewels, marbles, nuts, rocks, stones)

testosterone (tess-TOSS-tuh-roan). The male sex hormone, produced primarily in the testicles, which is responsible for the full development of the genitals and the secondary sex characteristics.

transsexual. A person who has a persistent sense of discomfort with his or her biological gender and may choose to undergo surgery to achieve the outward appearance of the other sex.

transvestite. One who derives sexual gratification from dressing in the clothing of the other sex.

tubal ligation (TOO-buhl lie-GAY-shun). A surgical procedure for sterilization in females. The fallopian tubes are cut, tied, sealed, or otherwise blocked off, either through an incision in the abdomen or through the vagina. Ova continue to be produced, but they are reabsorbed by the body. Commonly referred to as having one's tubes tied.

umbilical cord. The cord connecting the unborn infant to the placenta through which the fetus receives nourishment and passes waste materials.

urethra (yoo-REE-thruh). The duct through which urine passes out of the body from the bladder. In males, the urethra is also a part of the reproductive system, serving as a passageway for semen.

uterus. (YOO-tuhr-uhs). The muscular, hollow, pear-shaped organ in females in which babies grow and are nourished before birth. Also called the womb.

vagina. A passage leading from the uterus to the outside of the body. Receives the erect penis during sexual intercourse, and allows a baby to pass from the womb and out of the mother's body during delivery. Also referred to as the birth canal. (box, cunt)

vas deferens (VAZ DEHF-uhr-uhnz). The tube in the male through which sperm passes from the epididymis to the seminal vesicles and urethra. Also called the spermatic or sperm duct.

vasectomy (vah-SEHK-tuh-me). The surgical procedure for sterilization in males. On both sides of the scrotum, a small incision is made, and the sperm or duct or vas deferens is cut, tied, sealed, or otherwise blocked off. Normal ejaculation of semen continues, but the semen no longer contains sperm. Sperm continue to be produced, but they are reabsorbed by the body.

vulva (VUL-vuh). The external sex organ of the female. Includes the labia, clitoris, and the openings to the vagina and urethra. (beaver, pussy, snatch, slit, twat)

Recommended Resources

Books for Adults:

All About Sex: A Family Resource on Sex and Sexuality, by Ronald Filiberti Moglia, Ed.D. and Jon Knowles, Editors (Random House, 1997). Published by the Planned Parenthood Federation of America, this book offers information on sexuality and is designed to be used in families to stimulate communication about values and making responsible choices. (ISBN 0-609-80146-5) $20.00.

Embodiment: An Approach to Sexuality and Christian Theology, by James B. Nelson (Augsburg, 1990). A theological look at human sexuality. (ISBN 0-8066-1701-2) $19.99.

Five Hundred Questions Kids Ask About Sex and Some of the Answers, by Francis Younger (Charles C. Thomas Publisher, Ltd. 1992).

A Time to Speak: Faith Communities and Sexuality Education, by Debra W. Haffner (SIECUS, 1998).

Books for Children:

'Where Did I Come From?': The Facts of Life Without Any Nonsense and With Illustrations, by Peter Mayle (Carol Publishing Group, 1997). A classic book for children that uses humor and pictures to teach the basics of sex. A great book for reading together. (ISBN 0-8184-0591-3) $13.95.

A Better Safe Than Sorry Book: A Family Guide for Sexual Assault Prevention, by Sol and Judith Gordon (Prometheus Books, 1992). Designed to teach children aged three through nine how to prevent sexual assault. (ISBN 0-879757-68-X) $9.95.

Are You There, God? It's Me, Margaret, by Judy Blume (Laurel Leaf, 1991). A novel about a girl's anxieties over puberty. (ISBN 0-440-40419-6) $4.99.

Created by God: About Human Sexuality for Older Girls and Boys, written and edited by James H. Ritchie, Jr., Ed.D. (Abingdon, 1999). A reading book for older elementary children that doubles as a curriculum resource for group study; emphasizes Christian values, responsibility, relationships, and self-esteem along with comprehensive anatomical and physiological information. (ISBN 0-687-07409-6) $9.95.

Did the Sun Shine Before You Were Born?, by Sol and Judith Gordon and Sola Gordon (Prometheus Books, 1992). Exceptional realistic illustrations that include multi-racial children and children with disabilities. (ISBN 0-87975723-X) $9.95.

Facts About Sex for Today's Youth, by Sol Gordon (Prometheus Books, 1992). Brief; easy reading (fourth and fifth grade level). (ISBN 0-879757-71-X) $8.95.

How Babies Are Made, by Andrew C. Andry and Steven Schepp (Little Brown & Co., 1984). The story of reproduction in plants, animals, and humans. (ISBN 0-316-04227-7) $13.95.

Love and Sex in Plain Language, by Eric W. Johnson (Bantam Starfire, 1988). Informative book for 10-to-12-year-olds that stresses personal responsibility. (ISBN 0-553-47473-2) $14.99.

The Man Without a Face, by Isabelle Holland (HarperTrophy, 1993). A novel that deals with homosexuality. (ISBN 0-064-47028-8) $4.95.

No More Secrets for Me, by Oralee Wachter (Little Brown & Co., 1994). Four separate stories of children who are touched in ways they do not want to be touched; a sensitive treatment of a difficult subject. (ISBN 0-316-91491-6) $8.95.

Then Again, Maybe I Won't, by Judy Blume (Yearling Books, 1986). A novel about the problems faced by adolescent boys. (ISBN 0-440-48659-9) $4.50.

The What's Happening to My Body? Book for Boys: A Growing Up Guide for Parents and Sons, by Lynda Madaras and Ralph Lopez with Dane Saavedra; and *The What's Happening to My Body? Book for Girls: A Growing Up Guide for Parents and Daughters*, by Lynda Madaras, Area Madaras, and Cynthia W. Cooke (Newmarket Press, 1987). Two very comprehensive books that answer the questions children and youth have about their bodies. (ISBN 0-937858-99-4/boys; ISBN 0-937858-98-6/girls) $11.95.

Films, Filmstrips, and Videos:

"Talking About Sex: A Guide for Families" (Marketing Group, Planned Parenthood Federation of America, 1996). This is an animated video, parent guide, and activity book for young people (ages 10-14) that helps promote communication between children and parents on the subject of sex, puberty, and relationships. Kit: $29.95.

"Better Safe Than Sorry" (Vitascope-Filmfair, 1987). VHS/Beta, color, 17 minutes. 2nd edition. Stresses a child's responsibility for his or her own safety. $40 to rent; $345 to purchase.

"Better Safe Than Sorry II" (Vitascope-Filmfair, 1983). VHS/Beta, color, 15 minutes. Presents simple rules to help children prevent sexual abuse. $30 to rent, $260 to purchase.

Both of the above videos are available from Filmfair, 10900 Ventura, P.O. Box 1728, Studio City, CA 91604.

"A Family Talks About Sex" (Perennial, 1978). 16mm film, color, 29 minutes. Designed to help parents communicate. Available from EcuFilm; $20 to rent.

"Children and Sexuality" (Graded Press, 1989) VHS, color, 30 minutes. Developed as a companion video to this book. Psychologist and professor David Elkind helps parents and teachers prepare to teach children a Christian view of sexuality. $24.95.

"Kids Who Have Kids Are Kidding Themselves" (Educational Activities, 1979). 35mm filmstrip, color. Encourages responsibility in relationships. Available from Educational Activities, Box 392, Freeport, NY 11520; $30 to purchase.

"New Image Teen Theatre" (Planned Parenthood of San Diego, 1985). VHS, color, 30 minutes. Dramatizes communication on sexuality; winner of Alpha Award for Excellence in Children's Programming. Available from Printed Matter, Inc.; P.O. Box 15246; Atlanta, GA 30333. $20 to rent; $90 to purchase.

"Sex: A Topic for Conversation With Dr. Sol Gordon" (Mondell Productions, 1987). VHS/Beta. Three videos—for parents of young children, parents of teenagers, and for teenagers themselves. Humorous, using a question-and-answer format. Available from Mondell Productions, 5215 Homer St., Dallas, TX 75206. rental, $49 each; for purchase $99 each or $250 for all three.